THE GIRL WHO SMILED BEADS

THE GIRL WHO SMILED BEADS

*A Story of War
and What Comes After*

CLEMANTINE WAMARIYA

AND ELIZABETH WEIL

B \ D \ W \ Y
BROADWAY BOOKS
NEW YORK

Grateful acknowledgment is made to Random House, an imprint and
division of Penguin Random House LLC, for permission to reprint an
excerpt of "Still I Rise" from *And Still I Rise: A Book of Poems* by Maya
Angelou, copyright © 1978 by Maya Angelou. Reprinted by permission of
Random House, an imprint and division of Penguin Random House LLC.
All rights reserved.

Portions of this work first appeared in *Matter* (medium.com/matter),
as "Everything Is Yours, Everything Is Not Yours," on June 29, 2015.

Library of Congress Cataloging-in-Publication Data

Names: Wamariya, Clementine, author. | Weil, Elizabeth, 1969- author
Title: The girl who smiled beads : a story of war and what comes after /
   Clementine Wamariya and Elizabeth Weil.
Description: First edition. | New York : Crown Publishing, [2018]
Identifiers: LCCN 20170458714| ISBN 9780451495327 (hardcover) |
   ISBN 0451495322 (hardcover) | ISBN 9780451495334 (paperback) |
   ISBN 0451495330 (paperback) | ISBN 9780451495341 (ebook) |
   ISBN 0451495349 (ebook)
Subjects: LCSH: Wamariya, Clementine. | Rwanda--History--Civil War,
   1994--Refugees. | Refugees--Biography. | LCGFT: Autobiographies.
Classification: LCC DT450.437.W36 A3 2018 | DDC 967.57104/31 [B]
   --dc23 LC record available at https://lccn.loc.gov/2017045871

ISBN 978-0-451-49533-4
Ebook ISBN 978-0-451-49534-1

PRINTED IN THE UNITED STATES OF AMERICA

Map by Jeffrey L. Ward
Cover design by Michael Morris

10 9 8 7 6 5 4 3 2 1

First Paperback Edition

For Claire and for Mukamana, who taught me how
to create and live in my own umugani

A NOTE FROM THE AUTHORS

This is a work of nonfiction. A handful of the people in the book have been given pseudonyms; otherwise, everyone is identified by their real names. We have worked hard to be accurate and, just as crucial to a book like this, emotionally honest. But memory is flawed and idiosyncratic, and many of the events described here happened decades ago to a child under intense stress.

Every human life is equally valuable. Each person's story is vital. This is just one.

"What are the words you do not yet have? What do you need to say?"

—Audre Lorde, *Sister Outsider*

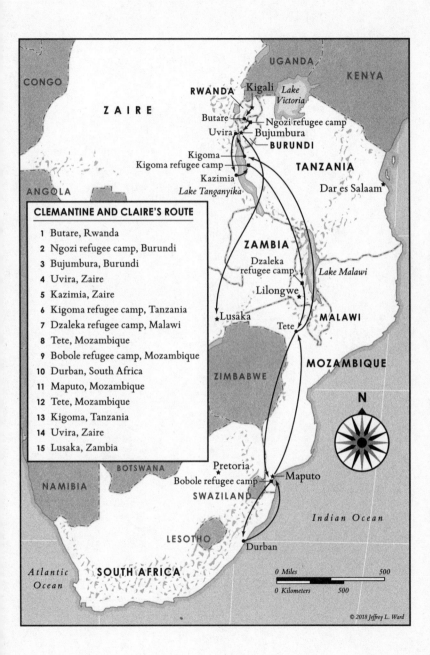

CONGO

UGANDA

KENYA

ZAIRE

RWANDA   Kigali   Lake Victoria

Butare

Ngozi refugee camp

Uvira   Bujumbura

BURUNDI

TANZANIA

Kigoma

Kigoma refugee camp

Kazimia

Lake Tanganyika   Dar es Salaam

ANGOLA

CLEMANTINE AND CLAIRE'S ROUTE

1   Butare, Rwanda
2   Ngozi refugee camp, Burundi
3   Bujumbura, Burundi
4   Uvira, Zaire
5   Kazimia, Zaire
6   Kigoma refugee camp, Tanzania
7   Dzaleka refugee camp, Malawi
8   Tete, Mozambique
9   Bobole refugee camp, Mozambique
10 Durban, South Africa
11 Maputo, Mozambique
12 Tete, Mozambique
13 Kigoma, Tanzania
14 Uvira, Zaire
15 Lusaka, Zambia

ZAMBIA

Dzaleka refugee camp

Lake Malawi

Lilongwe

Lusaka   Tete   MALAWI

ZIMBABWE   MOZAMBIQUE

N

BOTSWANA   Pretoria   Maputo

NAMIBIA   Bobole refugee camp

SWAZILAND

Indian Ocean

LESOTHO   Durban

Atlantic Ocean   SOUTH AFRICA

0 Miles   500

0 Kilometers   500

© 2018 Jeffrey L. Ward

PROLOGUE

The night before we taped the Oprah show, in 2006, I met my sister Claire at her apartment in a public housing unit in Edgewater, where she lived with the three kids she'd had before age twenty-two, thanks to her ex-husband, an aid worker who'd pursued her at a refugee camp. A black limo arrived and drove us to downtown Chicago, to the Omni Hotel, near where my sister used to work. I now can't think about that moment without also thinking about my own naïveté, but at the time all I felt was elated.

I was eighteen, a junior at New Trier High School, living Monday through Friday with the Thomas family in Kenilworth, a fancy suburb. I belonged to the church youth group. I ran track. I'd played Fantine in the school production of *Les Misérables*. I was whoever anybody wanted me to be.

Claire, meanwhile, remained steadfast, herself, a seemingly rougher bargain. Unlike me, she was not a child when we got resettled in the United States, so nobody sent her to school or took her in or filled her up with resources—piano lessons, speech therapists, cheerleading camp. Claire just kept hustling. For a while she made a living throwing parties, selling drinks and hiring DJs who mixed American hip-hop, the Zairean superstar Papa Wemba, and French rap. But then she learned it was illegal to sell liquor without a license and she started working full-time as a maid, cleaning two hundred hotel rooms a week.

All I knew about the show we were taping was that it was a two-part series: the first segment showed Oprah and Elie Wiesel visiting Auschwitz, God help us; the second featured the fifty winners of Oprah's high school essay contest. Like the other winners, I had written about Wiesel's book *Night,* his gutting story of surviving the Holocaust, and why it was still relevant today. The book disarmed me. I found it thrilling, and it made me ashamed. Wiesel had words that I did not have to describe the experiences of my early life.

I'd dictated my essay to Mrs. Thomas, as she sat in her tasteful Midwestern house—gracious lawn, mahogany floors—at a huge computer that took up the whole desk. "Clemantine," she'd said, "you have to enter. I just know you'll win." Mrs. Thomas had three children of her own, plus me. I called her "my American mother" and she called me "my African daughter." She packed my lunch every day and drove me to school.

In my essay I said that maybe if Rwandans had read *Night,* they wouldn't have decided to kill one another.

. . .

ON THE WAY TO DOWNTOWN Chicago, Claire and I had the inevitable conversation—*is this happening? this is so weird*—which was as close as my sister and I got to discussing what had happened to our lives. If we absolutely had to name our past in each other's presence, we'd call it "the war." But we tried not to do that, and that day we were both so consumed by all the remembering and willful forgetting that when we arrived at the Omni and the bellhop asked, "Do you have any bags?" we realized we'd left all our clothes at home.

Claire took the L back to her apartment, where a friend was watching her children—Mariette, who was almost ten; Freddy, who was eight; and Michele, who was five. I stayed in the hotel room, lost.

Harpo Studios gave us each a $150 stipend for dinner. It was more than Claire's monthly food stamp allowance. When Claire returned we ordered room service. We woke at 4:00 a.m. and spent hours getting dressed.

THAT DAY, FOR THE SHOW, the producers directed us to the huge studio. Oprah sat onstage on a white love seat, next to tired old Elie Wiesel in a white overstuffed chair. He was alive, old but alive, which meant the world to me. He kept looking at the audience, like he had a lot to say but there was no time to say it.

In this nice studio, in front of all these well-dressed people, Oprah's team played the video of Oprah and Elie Wiesel walking arm in arm through snow-covered Auschwitz, discussing the Holocaust.

Then the producers gave us a break. We sat in silence. Some of us were horrified and others were crying.

After that, Oprah said glowing things about all the winners of the essay contest except me. I told myself this was fine. Fine. I hadn't really gone to school until age thirteen, and when I was seven I'd celebrated Christmas in a refugee camp in Burundi with a shoebox of pencils that I'd buried under our tent so that nobody would steal it. Being in the audience was enough, right? Plus, I kept wanting to say to Oprah: *Do you know how many years, and across how many miles, Claire has been talking about meeting you?*

But then Oprah leaned forward and said, "So, Clemantine, before you left Africa, did you ever find your parents?"

I had a mike cord tucked under my black TV blazer and a battery pack clipped to my black TV pants, so I should have suspected something like this was coming. "No," I said. "We tried UNICEF . . . , we tried everywhere, walking around, searching and searching and searching."

"So when was the last time you saw them?" she asked.

"It was 1994," I said, "when I had no idea what was going on."

"Well, I have a letter from your parents," Oprah said, as though we'd won a game show. "Clemantine and Claire, come on up here!"

CLAIRE HELD ON TO ME. She was shaking, but she kept on her toughest, most skeptical face, because she knows more about the world than I do, and also because she refused to think, even after all we'd been through, that anybody was better or more important than she was. When we were dirt poor and alone, she'd be in her seventh hour of scrubbing someone's laundry by hand and she'd see on a TV an image of Angelina Jolie, swaggering and gleaming, radiating moral superiority, and even then Claire would say, "Who is that? God? You, you're human. Nothing separates me from you."

I have never been Claire. I have never been inviolable. Often, still, my own life story feels fragmented, like beads unstrung. Each time I scoop up my memories, the assortment is slightly different. I worry, at times, that I'll always be lost inside. I worry that I'll be forever confused. But that day I leapt up onto the set, smiling. One of the most valuable skills I'd learned while trying to survive as a refugee was reading what other people wanted me to do.

"This is from your family, in Rwanda," Oprah said, handing me a tan envelope. She looked solemn, confident in her purpose. "From your father and your mother and your sisters and your brother."

Claire and I did know that our parents were alive. We knew they'd lost everything—my father's business, my mother's garden—and that they now lived in a shack on the outskirts of Kigali. We talked to them on the phone, but only rarely because—how do you start? *Why didn't you look harder for us? How are you? I'm fine, thanks. I've been working at the Gap and I've found it's much easier to learn to read English if you also listen to audiobooks.*

I opened the envelope and pulled out a sheet of blue paper. Then Oprah put her hand on mine to stop me from unfolding the letter. It was a huge relief. I didn't want to have a breakdown on TV.

"You don't have to read it right now, in front of all these people," Oprah said. "You don't have to read it in front of all these people . . ." She paused. "Because . . . because . . . your family . . . IS HERE!"

I started walking backward. Claire's jaw unhinged in a caricature of shock. Then a door that had images of barbed wire on it—created especially for this particular episode, I assume, to evoke life in an internment camp—opened stage right and out came an eight-year-old boy, who was apparently my brother. He was followed by my father, in a dark suit, salmon shirt, and tie; a shiny new five-year-old sister; my mother in a long blue dress; and my sister Claudette, now taller than me. I'd last seen her when she was two years old and I still believed my mother had picked her up from the fruit market.

I'd fantasized about this moment so many times. In Malawi, I used to write my name in dust on trucks, hoping my mother would see my loopy cursive *Clemantine* and realize that I was alive. In Zaire, I'd saved coins so I could buy my parents presents. In Tanzania, I'd collected marbles for my older brother, Pudi, who wasn't there for this reunion. Pudi was dead.

Claire remained frozen for a moment. So I, in my TV clothes and blown-out hair, ran toward my Oprah-produced family, arms outstretched. I hugged my brother. I hugged my father. I hugged my tiny little sister. I hugged my mother, but my knees gave out and she had to pick me up. Then I hugged her. I hugged Claudette, my little sister, little no more. I walked across the stage and hugged Oprah. I hugged lovely, weathered Elie Wiesel.

The cameras were so far away that I forgot I was participating in a million-viewer spectacle, that my experience, my joy and pain, were being consumed by the masses, though I was aware enough to realize that everybody in the audience was crying.

A FEW HOURS LATER, THOUGH it seemed like minutes, we found ourselves on the sidewalk outside the studio, and my family took a black limo north to my sister's apartment. She lived in the front unit of a squat brick low-rise, across the street from the L tracks and a block away from an abandoned wooden house with a gable roof, a once fantastic, now forgotten home that I hoped would someday be ours. I would put everybody in it. We would be a family again.

Nobody talked in the car. In the apartment, nobody knew what to do either. My mother, in her long blue dress, kept sitting down and standing up and touching everything—the living room walls, the TV remote—and singing about how God had protected us and now we must serve and love him. My father kept smiling, as though someone he mistrusted were taking pictures of him. Claire remained nearly catatonic: rocking, stone-faced. I thought she'd finally gone crazy, for real.

I sat on Claire's couch, looking at my strange new siblings, the ones who'd replaced me and Claire. They looked so perfect, their skin unblemished, their eyes alight, like an excellent fictional representation of a family that could have been mine. But they didn't know me and I didn't know them, and the gap between us was a billion miles wide.

I fell asleep crying on Mariette's bed and woke still wearing my Oprah shoes.

THE NEXT DAY WAS FRIDAY. Of course, I didn't go to school. We needed to start making up for so much lost time. Yet I couldn't look at my parents—they were ghosts.

I felt gratitude, yes. Oprah had brought my parents to me. But I also felt kicked in the stomach, as though my life were some psychologist's perverse experiment: *Let's see how far we can take a person down, and then how far we can raise her up, and then let's see what happens!*

Saturday, my family, along with the Thomases, drove up the lakeshore to the Chicago Botanic Garden, where we stared at the Illinois lilies and roses. We all wanted these to be beautiful links to the lilies and roses in Kigali, threads knitting this present to that past, but everything was awkward, and it felt as though cameras were still following us around. Sunday we did Navy Pier—the gaudy Ferris wheel, the sticky cotton candy, all the tourist stuff.

My father kept smiling his fake, pained smile. Mine probably looked the same: a smile covering a scream. Claire barely said a word. Then, Monday morning, my parents and new siblings left on the flight back to Rwanda that Oprah's people had booked for them, and Mrs. Thomas picked me up as usual at Claire's apartment. I had no idea how to make sense of what had just happened. So I just ran out to her Mercedes and she dropped me off at school.

1

When I was a regular child, I lived in Kigali, Rwanda, and I was a precocious snoop. My nickname was Cassette. I repeated everything I saw or heard, including that my sister Claire, who was nine years older than me, wore shorts under her skirt and played soccer instead of doing family errands after school.

When she did follow directions—go buy tomatoes, pick up six Cokes for guests—she spent only a quarter of the money my mother gave her, because Claire, even at fourteen, could look out for herself. She understood value. She knew confidence was currency. She realized that if she told the tomato vendor she'd pay him less today but return every week and buy only from him, he'd accept the bargain, she'd pocket some money, and they'd both walk away happy.

She also knew life was harder and more costly when I

tagged along. I talked too much. I tattled. I asked too many questions. I also had a lisp and was difficult to understand. Claire made fun of me, how my tongue got in the way. She told me to repeat words, and laughed.

We lived in a gray stucco ranch house on a gravel road, up the hill from the market, near one of the few tennis courts in the city. The houses in our neighborhood sat close together, each with a red roof and fenced with creosote bushes, thick and dense, and trimmed weekly into tidy partitions.

In our backyard was an outdoor kitchen, with a big sandbox in which my mother buried carrots and sweet potatoes to shield them from the heat and make them even sweeter. In the front yard stood a mango tree, old and wet, with sturdy leaves. You could sit in it and it would hug you. Every day when we came home from school, Pudi and I climbed up and stood in the branches, in what was then my whole world, shaking the leaves, pretending the tree was a bus that would take us to Butare, where our grandmother lived, about three hours away, or even to Canada.

My mother was short and curvy and regal and poised, with high cheekbones, like my grandparents, and bright white teeth with gaps between them, which Rwandans consider beautiful. We have a word for it in Kinyarwanda: *inyinya*. She'd fallen in love with my father and they'd decided to marry against his family's wishes.

My mother spent her mornings at church, just up the hill, and her afternoons in the garden, which was her Eden. There she taught me the names of plants—cauliflower, bird-of-paradise—and how to care for each, which ones needed to be in the cool soil under the mango tree and which needed direct sun. She grew oranges, lemons, guava, and papaya; hibiscus, plumeria, sanchezia, anthurium, geraniums, and peonies. I would pluck the stamens off the tiger lilies and rest them above my lip, the orange pollen leaving a bright powdered mustache.

Saturdays my mother dragged me, Pudi, and Claire to clean the homes of old people. The old people were so cranky. They yelled at us if we ate the fruit that had fallen off their mango trees. My mother didn't care if they were mean.

She also took in girls from the country, young women who, before they married, wanted to spend a year or two in a big city with malls, office buildings, cathedrals, and paved roads, earn a little money, and see the world. These women worked as nannies, or they helped in the kitchen, or they cleaned and laundered clothes. My mother insisted that Claire and I learn how to do these chores alongside them. We were never to think we were better. I didn't mind the work. I wanted order in my world. Even at four, I was compulsively neat, straightening the shoes by the door and resweeping the slate in the courtyard.

Claire hated housework. She did not want to be slowed down. She had big plans and could not wait to break free—to go to college in Canada, where many Rwandans dreamed of moving because it was like America except that they spoke French. French was the second language Rwandans learned in school, as the Belgians had colonized Rwanda. If not Canada, Claire wanted to travel to Europe—anything to live in *iburayi*, Rwandans' all-purpose expression for "abroad" or "away." Claire had a godmother who lived in Montreal who sent her the most fabulous gifts:

a watch with a silver band, a green rain set with matching slicker, umbrella, and boots.

My dreams, at age four, were far less adventurous. I wanted to be fed ice cream and pineapple cakes. I wanted to wear a teal-blue school uniform and grow into Claire's clothes.

MY MOTHER DRESSED TIDILY, MODESTLY, always, as if to say, *I'm here but I'm not here. Don't look at me.* She wore a T-shirt and bright *kitenge,* or long wrapper, to garden, and a long pleated skirt with a high-necked blouse and sensible black low-heeled shoes to church. Her heels never made noise. She never wore makeup, only a bit of Vaseline to brighten her lips. She'd absorbed the potent Catholic-Rwandan-postcolonial ethos: You want to stay as invisible as possible. You don't want eyes on you. Mastering that was my job growing up: to learn how to be proper, how to be quiet. I was an unenthusiastic student.

Many of our neighbors' families were exuberant and different—Muslim instead of Catholic, Zairean instead of Rwandan. I wanted to taste how they prepared their beans and study the designs on their plates. I wanted to celebrate Ramadan and the Indian holiday Diwali. Some days, when I visited neighbors' homes, I picked through their bedrooms and bathrooms, looking at their hairbrushes, toothbrushes, medicines, and soaps. I wanted to know their secrets—not the deep dark ones, the little human ones. I wanted to know what their bodies were like.

My mother would try to discourage my curiosity, reproaching me with the words *ushira isoni*—you are not shy.

Rwandans, especially girls, were supposed to be reserved, contained, nearly opaque. When I walked with my mother into town, I'd point to each house and ask, "Who lives there? How many kids? Is anybody sick?" I didn't fit in.

One day, when she was in her kitenge in the garden, she heard on the radio that a friend had died, or *kwitaba imana*—the idiom means "responded to God." She started to cry. That was the first and only time I saw my mother cry. Adults in Rwanda do not cry. Children can cry until they learn to speak. Then it's time to stop. If you absolutely must cry after that, you have to cry like you're singing, like a melancholy bird.

I begged my mother to let me go to the funeral. I wanted to know how funerals worked. My nanny, Mukamana, who I loved and adored, ironed my best cotton dress and buttoned me into it, and I took my mother's hand as we walked down the gravel road and across the bridge toward town.

Rwanda is all hills. Mukamana said that the creator, Imana, hadn't wanted to stretch out the land, as he wanted Rwanda to be unique. Near the church, we joined fifty people sitting on long benches arranged in a rectangle under a tree. Everybody was silent or whispering. My mother, like the rest of the adults, remained calm and composed. I sat there, staring at the adults' faces, very confused.

I did not hear God talking to anybody. I just heard a priest offering comfort, some hymns. After the service I asked a few of my mother's friends if they'd heard or seen God, and they took my hands in theirs and patted them, as if to say, *You'll understand soon enough.*

But soon enough was too far off. I wanted to understand

right then. In my short life, death was an idle threat, a sibling's joke—Pudi or Claire saying our mother would kill me if I picked too many roses. My mother did her Rwandan best to explain. She told me death was a welcoming home. But I felt aggrieved, even insulted, by the obvious oversimplification of what it meant to die. In my four-year-old imperiousness, I believed I could handle the truth. I thought I deserved to know. I demanded it.

After the funeral I spent as much time as possible around old, sick people. I tagged along with my mother when she went to read them scripture. I wanted to listen for God talking to them, calling them home. Did a person need to respond to God when God called? What if you wanted to live? If God was just extending an invitation, you could decline, right? You could say *no thank you* and stay where you were.

MY DAYS WERE FILLED WITH the indignations of being young and spoiled. I hated the lotion my nanny applied after my bath. I hated my bathrobe. I wanted the robe with buttons, like Claire's, and if not that, I wanted to be allowed to dress like Pudi. Pudi's given name was Claude and his nickname came from his love of Puma and Adidas. My mother indulged him by letting him wear his bright red Adidas soccer jersey under his school uniform, even though the jersey smelled.

Daily, maybe hourly, I begged Mukamana to tell me stories to help me make sense of the world, like that the gods shook out the ocean like a rug to make waves. My favorite was that there was a beautiful, magical girl who roamed the earth, smiling beads. When Mukamana told me this story, she said, "What do you think happened next?" and whatever I said, whatever future I imagined, Mukamana would make come true. Mukamana wrapped her long, curly hair in a magnificent cloth, and she slept in my room with me, each of us on our own bed. She taught me songs to get me through my morning ritual: rise, pray for the day, make my bed, brush my teeth, wash my face, fix my hair, get dressed, greet everyone.

I refused to do anything until she told me a story, and she used my desire to get the upper hand. "Well, if you take a nap, I'll tell you a story. If you don't do it then I won't tell you."

Growing up, I wanted to be like her. I wanted to tell stories and dance for others like she would do for me. All Mukamana's stories involved singing and dancing, tapping out rhythms with her feet. Her stories never had set endings. She always asked, "And then what do you think happened? Can you guess what happened next?" She was the only one willing to help me understand why the sky was so high, or where water first came from.

MY FATHER OWNED A CAR service. He built the business gradually, like any good entrepreneur: first one car, then two, then a small fleet of minibuses, and by the time I was born a big commercial garage on a busy street that smelled like car oil and dust.

He was solid, thick-chested, broad-shouldered, with a

wide forehead and a broad smile, plus ears that stuck out just enough to take off his intimidating edge. He worked long hours. I didn't see him much. On the evenings he was home, I fought with Claire over who would bring him his leather slippers. Claire knew this was the best time to ask for money or new Nikes. I wanted to trade his slippers for a taste of his beer.

My father worked so hard to build this—a middle-class home. When my parents married, they didn't have enough money to throw a wedding. Now, some afternoons, if it was hot or business was slow, my father came home to nap. I knew that I was meant to be quiet while he slept, to stop playing and screaming in the garden, especially near his open window. But one afternoon Pudi and I started playing in the mango tree and I forgot.

Discipline was usually my mother's province. She was strict and understated. When we misbehaved, she made us kneel in the corner and face the wall, sometimes holding stones over our heads. It was awful. When someone in the family lied—usually it was me—my mother would boil water and have all of us sit around the pot. "If you're dishonest and you put your hand in there, it will burn," she said. "If you didn't do it, your hand will be just fine." One of us always confessed.

Claire hated my mother's punishments more than the rest of us. They enraged her and filled her with shame. "Why don't you just beat us, like everybody else?" she asked our mother.

But that afternoon, when my father came home to nap and I neglected to be quiet, it wasn't my mother who punished me. It was my father. He opened the window, called me into the den, and smacked me in the face. I can still feel the heat. I peed on myself.

That was the most cruelty I'd ever seen.

WHEN I WAS FIVE, I started kindergarten. By then I had a new baby sister. I felt threatened, as all older siblings do, and begged every day for my mother to return her. I considered running away.

Kindergarten was a privilege. Neither Claire nor Pudi had gone, as my parents hadn't had the money when they were little. My school was beautiful, nestled on the hillside, with a glamorous teacher who wore high heels that clicked against the hallway floor. The place smelled like crayons. We sang, made clay bowls and mugs, and ate lunch in the shade.

Each day, with my lunch, I carried a green thermos of milk tea. I considered myself the most special child there, maybe the most special child in all Rwanda, because one day Mukamana picked me up carrying the green umbrella, slicker, and rain boots that had belonged to Claire. It was monsoon season, warm and pouring. I slipped on Claire's green boots, and I begged Mukamana to take the long way home, around the next hill through town, not directly over the bridge. I wanted to be a one-girl parade showing off my posh rain gear.

But Mukamana told me that we couldn't take the long way because it was flooded. I was furious.

I forgave her only when I found Pudi waiting to play. The rainwater was gushing off our red roof into the slate courtyard. He stole the soap from the kitchen and slicked up the slate. We ran and slid until my mother snapped and demanded that we come inside.

Shortly after that, Mukamana disappeared. I asked my mother why and she said the *intambara*—the conflict. That word had no meaning to me, no story attached.

ANOTHER NANNY ARRIVED, PASCAZIA, and she was not Mukamana, so I hated her. She did not tell me stories the way Mukamana had. She did not wrap her hair in an elegant cloth. One day, Pascazia came to pick me up at kindergarten in the rain, and she did not bring the green rain boots and slicker.

On our way home, we passed a group of men singing and dancing in the street. They were sweaty, carrying green, gold, and red flags. It looked so festive, like a carnival. I was entranced by the large drum. A dozen pickup trucks were parked by the side of the road, with a crowd gathering behind them to watch. I wanted to stop and sing and dance with the men, and usually Pascazia was happy to dawdle. She liked to ply me with *mandazi,* or beignets, so I was always patient while she talked to her friends. Now I begged for *mandazi* so I would at least get to join the crowd and stare. She refused.

The next week, just before we crossed the bridge and were starting up the hill to our house, we saw a crowd in a circle. People said someone was getting stoned for stealing. I didn't understand what was happening. There were more flags, red, black, yellow, and green, and more singing and marching. I was transfixed. Mukamana had told me an old story once, about men fighting each other with spears, up in the hills. Those spears left many broken hearts and broken bodies. The broken men, she'd said, still lived in hiding. Were we among those men, in those hills, now? I asked Pascazia. She yanked my arm. She made us leave.

At home I tattled to my mother. I didn't know what I'd seen, but I'd been mesmerized and I knew that my seeing it was wrong.

"Where did you go? Why did you pass?" my mother said to Pascazia, a sharp rebuke. Her lips pulled tight over the gap in her teeth. She almost never raised her voice. "You shouldn't have walked that way."

A few days later Pascazia disappeared. I never went to kindergarten again.

YOU KNOW THOSE LITTLE PELLETS you drop in water that expand into huge sponges? My life was the opposite. Everything shrank.

First I was forbidden to play in the mango tree. Pudi tried to entertain me in the house, fake-reading to me in French. He was supposed to be learning French in school but he never studied. So we just looked in the books at the pictures of Tintin, and Pudi made up stories. We traveled together to the jungle with Milou, Tintin's dog. A lion would appear and we'd escape to the caves.

Next I was forbidden to play with my friend Neglita. She was my oldest playmate, one of my few friends my age, and I thought she was perfect. We made up fairy worlds. She let me set the rules. We collected petals and bits of moss, and the fairies wore the petals as dresses and lived in the moss.

Not long before the stoning, my mother had walked me to Neglita's house to play. On the way we gathered seed-pods, and in Neglita's yard she and I set the pods on hot rocks and waited for them to pop. I slept over at Neglita's house that night, and when my mother came in the morning I didn't want to leave. As a sort of promise, she suggested that I lend a sweater to Neglita and that I take one of hers home. That way we would have a reason to see each other soon, to trade our sweaters back. Neglita's sweater was blue and smelled like eucalyptus. I wanted mine back, but I never saw Neglita again.

The radio was now on all the time, a horrendous hiss. Pudi took me to see *Rambo,* screened on a bedsheet at a neighbor's house. I had never seen a gun fired, let alone real combat. I was so scared that I ran home alone without my shoes. After that, all the kids in the neighborhood became obsessed with *Rambo.* They cut their T-shirts into tank tops and wore bandannas on their foreheads. The boys found sticks and hid behind trees and pretended to shoot.

Houses were robbed, simply to prove that they could be robbed. The robbers left notes demanding oil, or sugar, or a TV. I asked adults to explain, but their faces had turned to concrete, and they nudged me back into childish concerns. Sometimes the men left grenades—that's what I heard, though I didn't really know what a grenade was. I just knew they could cut you into a hundred pieces. I thought there must be hundreds of tiny fires inside. How else could one blow up a whole body? That little thing, that much power?

. . .

SOME DAYS THE WORLD FELT GREEN, some days it felt yellow, but never a happy yellow.

All the girls who lived with my family returned to their hometowns. The only person who worked at the house now was a security guard, who stood in the front garden and smoked cigarettes in the evening while my father was at work. When my father returned home I still brought him his slippers and he still gave me a sip of his beer. But he listened to the radio and there was no wide smile. Just *here's a sip, be quiet.*

Our curtains, which my mother had always thrown open at five each morning, suddenly remained closed. The drumming started up again, loud and far away. Then the car horns. My father stopped working after dark. My mother saw men, not boys, wearing *Rambo*-style boots and marching near the church. She stopped going to church. Instead she prayed in my room, where my siblings now slept sometimes, because it had the smallest window.

No one came over for dinner anymore. My mother served carrots and lentils, so many carrots and lentils. The potatoes she once used for stews came from the market, and nobody in my family went to the market anymore.

The electricity flickered on and off. The water stopped working. There was shushing, so much shushing, so much pressure to be quiet and still. *Checkeka*—shush, be silent. My parents said *checkeka* to me a hundred times a day.

There were more nights than days. I cried when the sun went down. Someone left a grenade at our neighbor's house. By then I was six.

Soon after that, my uncle died. That's what my mother said: *He died*. I asked if he was called to God and she said no. I heard conversations I didn't understand about *them* coming. *Them*—always *them,* plural, spoken with a hiss. Guests had always been important. Guests were special. When guests arrived my mother put out roasted nuts and Coke. *Them* was not guests.

We sat in the house. Lights off. Everyone prayed, but nobody talked. No more teasing from Claire and Pudi that I was adopted, no more fearmongering that when my tooth fell out a new one wouldn't grow in its place. There was nothing—no parable for the world closing in on itself, no fantastical story like the sky kissing the ground to make the morning dew.

Nobody tried to explain anything at all, except Pudi, who on occasion would step out of his *Rambo* fantasy to make up ridiculous tales: *There's this one bird who takes chickens and babies and little kids, and that's why you can't be outside at noon. If it's thundering you can't wear red, because if you wear red that's a target for the thunder to eat you up.*

It thundered a lot in those days. Every time we heard an explosion Pudi said, *That's thunder,* and when I looked confused he added, *Haven't you heard thunder when it's not raining?* He told me that if anything worse than thunder happened, I should climb up into the space between the ceiling and the roof. It would take a long time for anybody to find me there.

My parents' faces turned into faces I had never seen. I heard noises that I did not understand—not screaming, worse. My mother cried again. My parents whispered and I eavesdropped. I heard them say that some robbers had ransacked yet another neighbor's house. They stole their money, tore their pictures from the walls, destroyed their furniture and lit it on fire. They nailed a note to the front door saying they'd soon return for their girls.

THEN ONE DAY MY MOTHER told me and Claire to pack a few things to go to my grandmother's farm in Butare, a few hours south, toward the Burundi border. Claire loved it there and I loved it there and we revered our grandmother. She lived in an adobe-style house with small windows, a thatched roof, and rows and rows of sunflowers behind it—a house out of a fairy tale. I felt free there and never wore shoes. After the previous war, my grandmother had returned to her land with her five children, including my mother, the second daughter. My grandfather had stayed behind in Uganda.

A friend of my father's arrived in a van early the next morning. It was still dark. I wanted to show my grandmother a ceramic mug I'd made at school. I asked my mother to take it off the shelf where she kept our artwork, but she insisted I leave it behind. I was furious. My mother didn't care. She just handed me a bag of clothes and put me in the van alongside Claire and made me promise to behave. As we left she said, "Please do not talk."

On the way out of Kigali, we stopped to pick up two of my cousins, girls Claire's age. Their father, my uncle, was the one who had died but had not been called to God. The driver knocked on the door. Nobody came out. We stopped at other houses; other girls entered the van.

We all squished together in the middle of the bench seats, away from the windows. Sometimes we crouched on the floor. We rode up and over the hills, the curved slopes soft, like a body, past the stands of trees, the rice paddies, the hibiscus flowers, the homes with the red roofs and the homes with the tin roofs, the university.

The ride took forever. Claire insisted we play the silent game whenever I asked a question. We didn't eat kabobs or buy the soap that we always brought to my grandmother as a gift. We didn't even stop to use the bathroom.

In Butare, when we arrived, some of my cousins were already in my grandmother's kitchen, the older girls peeling potatoes like city girls—not well. I idolized these cousins, their black freckles and fancy clothes. Now my grandmother circled my cousins like a lion, livid, determined to keep her pride safe and together. Earlier that day they'd snuck out of her house and walked down the red dirt road to borrow a neighbor's dry-skin lotion.

Every hour I demanded an update on when my parents were coming, or at least my brother, Pudi. I missed him. My grandmother, cousins, and sister all just said, "Soon." Nobody would play with me. I felt outraged at my mistreatment. I stopped eating and bathing and refused to let anyone touch my hair. After a few nights my grandmother took me, Claire, and my cousins to a different house to sleep.

The following night she took us outside and told us to climb inside the deep pit in the ground reserved for burying the wooden cask she used to make banana wine. Colors and sounds bloomed, then exploded around me. I didn't sleep.

. . .

WHEN IT HAPPENED, WE HEARD a knock on the door. My grandmother gestured for us to be silent—*checkeka check-eka checkeka*. Then she motioned for us to run, or really to belly-crawl, out past the beaming sunflowers through the sweet potato field.

I carried a rainbow blanket, which turned out to be a towel. Claire pulled my arm. The earth felt soft and lumpy, a bucket of broken chalk. Once we reached the tall trees we ran, for real, off the farm, out of the ordered rows, and deep into a thick banana grove, where we saw other people, most of them young, some of them bloody with wounds.

I had so many questions. The cuts looked too large, too difficult to accomplish, gaping mouths on midnight skin. Claire shut down. It could have been a second, it could have been forever.

We walked for hours, until everything hurt, not toward anything, just away. We rubbed the red-brown mud and eucalyptus leaves on our bodies so we could disappear. Prickers grated my ankles. We walked up and over and around and down, so many hills. We heard laughing and screaming and pleading and crying and then cruel laughing again.

I didn't know how to name the noises. They were human and not human. I never learned the right words in Kinyarwanda. I hope they don't exist. But without words my mind had no way to define or understand the awful sounds, nowhere to store them in my brain. It was cold and green and wet and then bushes and my legs were shaking and eyes, so many eyes.

My thoughts and senses became jumbled. Time felt hot. Silence was dizzying. My fear was bright blue.

. . .

WE NEEDED TO LISTEN, SO we avoided roads and walked instead only on the little paths animals used to pass through the scrub. If we heard any noise we crouched and froze.

Claire's face—I'd never seen anything like it. I couldn't look at her eyes. We stopped and knelt by a stream to drink. I started to shiver, despite the heat. I said to Claire, "I want to go home." She stood up, pulled my wrist, and said, "We can't stay here. Other people will come."

I held on to Claire's shirt, too exhausted to hold hands. We passed a few people. One woman tried to give us food, but we were too afraid to take it. You could tell who was running from their swollen feet, the rips in their clothes, their bleeding knees.

A man told us he knew the way to safety. We followed him to the Burundi border, to the Akanyaru River. There were bodies floating in it. I still didn't understand what killing was. To me, the people in the river were sleeping. People in water sleeping and sleeping. That's all I knew.

We walked until late afternoon, almost dusk. We didn't know where we were going—just to the next hill and then the hill after that and then the hill after that and then across another river. We saw more bodies, sleeping and sleeping. I stopped thinking about my feet and worried about finding a place to rest.

That night the world ripped in two. The sky opened and out gushed a rain so heavy and complete there was no point trying to hide from it. Thunder shook the earth and made our legs wobble. We were pelted by hail.

For a while I could hear Claire asking God why this needed to be happening, why he was testing us this way. But then she stopped. Our mother had told us that hell was a fire that never ends, and that this hellfire was fed by the wood and charcoal of each of our sins. This was hell, clearly, but the wrong hell. Claire stopped speaking aloud to God.

Near dawn we found a house with its front door ripped off. The place was the darkest bedlam, the detritus from its own storm. We hid under the bed all day.

All my toenails fell out. We lived on fruit. Days were for hiding, nights for walking. I thought I was one hundred years old. I thought I was the thunder's child. I had always wanted to be Claire's age or my mother's. I knew I was six. Age made no sense anymore.

I HELD ON TO MY TOWEL. I looked out for stray dogs. We found a school, a long narrow building with a row of tiny open windows across its front. The school had a playground—that felt comforting. Other people were hiding inside the school. The people's faces were all eyes— wide, scared, wild, sharp. The windows had no panes and no shutters, and I wished they did.

We stayed in the school all afternoon. A woman began crying in agony. She could not stop. At dusk, the sky turned bright orange. Pudi had told me the sky turned that color when a nun or priest died. We left at dark to walk. The crickets were so loud.

After days, a week—I could not keep track—we found a cornfield where we heard children playing. Their cries now sounded exotic to me, as the whole world had changed. Claire and I exchanged no words. Our mouths, our bodies, had gone mute. Only our eyes still could speak and even then only in bursts. I could see, and then I stopped seeing, the lights flickering in my mind. We crouched down to hide among the giant cornstalks. We each shucked a few cobs and tried to eat the kernels. They tasted like paste from school.

Claire decided that we needed to find the playing children's parents, so we left the field and started walking down a red-brown dirt road. We saw some farmers. Claire approached a woman, her leathered skin loose and pleated over her strong arms. Claire told her that we'd come from over the hill.

The woman asked Claire about our family. Claire's eyes did not flicker. She said, "Our family will follow soon."

The woman accepted this non-explanation. She sensed there would be no real answer. She said she'd keep us until our parents arrived. Then she whistled to some men cutting sugarcane across the road. They gave us thick, sweet lengths and plastic bottles of water and stared at us like we'd risen from the dead.

I felt ripped out of the ground—not ready to be transplanted, just destroyed.

"You can't trust anyone," Claire whispered. "Don't tell her anything."

THE WOMAN TOOK US TO her one-room hut, where she slept with her husband and four children on a bed of straw. They were so poor. They had their corn, a few sweet potatoes, and a line of pineapple trees. They farmed, kept a portion of the food for themselves, and sold the rest, which was not much, to the ministry down the road.

All night I itched. In the morning I woke with welts and the woman's children laughed at me for not knowing what lice were.

We stayed there, working in the fields and eating boiled corn and sweet potatoes with no oil or salt—the worst cooked food I'd ever consumed. We slept when their kids slept and ate when their kids ate. The fields were in a valley and the hut was on a hill, so when we finished farming we ran up to the hut to watch the road. I imagined my mother or my father or my grandmother coming. I cried until I couldn't cry anymore. I only knew lives like this existed from stories—lives without mattresses, lives with rats. I was ready to be found, ready to go, not to live like this.

After a few weeks, we saw people walking down the roads, hundreds, maybe thousands, carrying bags, children, baskets. One man carried a dog. Claire decided we needed to join them.

"What if you go and you don't find anything?" the hut mother asked. She wrapped some sweet potatoes in a sweater and handed it to Claire.

Claire said, "We need to go."

IT'S STRANGE, HOW YOU GO from being a person who is away from home to a person with no home at all. The place that is supposed to want you has pushed you out. No other place takes you in. You are unwanted, by everyone. You are a refugee.

We kept walking, now with this crowd. Through forests and up hills that felt like mountains. The sound of the group was the sound of children crying for their mothers. *Mama. Ma-MA. Mama mama mama.* I did not say it myself. I did not dare. That sound filled my brain and never drained.

We walked, this mass of desperation, no longer distinct people. We walked until we stopped and fell asleep. While trying to sleep I heard people asking, "Have you seen my daughter?" "Do you know Umutoni?" It was so loud.

We walked over a hill, through a forest, to a large clearing, or what became a clearing when our mass pushed down the young limber trees. We stopped there. The adults decided this would be our home. You could walk a mile and find a stream of water. You could walk toward town and ask the farmers to share whatever they had, though they also had nothing. If they were not there you took a few sweet potatoes or some corn, and in return you left a sweet potato vine or a shirt, to let the farmer know that you recognized taking his food was wrong. You'd just run out of choices.

The crying. The moaning. The faces. The expressions of pain. I did not ask questions. I was glad we did not have a mirror. I wanted to think I still had the same face.

The clearing became a colony and people started dying. I had never seen that many flies and bugs of all kinds, day in and day out. Cholera, dysentery, infected wounds. People bonded together into groups for safety. *You have daughters, I have daughters. You're young, we're young.* Nobody spoke of the past or the future. Time balled up into a knot.

We stuck with the young people with daughters and moved across the clearing when our patch turned to mud.

. . .

ONE NIGHT I WOKE UP. The stars and the moon glowed as though nothing bad had occurred. Bodies were scattered everywhere, lifeless, yet alive.

I tiptoed away to pee and when I returned I couldn't find Claire. She always slept on her side with her elbow folded under her ear. I couldn't find her shape. I moved from one body to the next, crouching down, tapping faces.

I woke a woman with her head resting on a *kanga* cloth, her cotton blouse the same color as the dirt. She had a young baby. I asked her to help me find my sister.

She patted her *kanga. Sleep here,* she said. *Let's wait for daylight.*

I shook my head, refused.

She stood up, collected her baby, and walked with me around the clusters of bodies. We didn't find Claire. I cried until I felt empty and I thought of all the bad things that might happen to me if I did not find my sister. I would be an orphan. I would be forever lost. No one would know that I wanted the bathrobe with the buttons. No one would know that Mukamana had to sing me a song to get me to brush my teeth.

The woman with the dirt-red shirt and the baby was so bone-tired and calm. She tried her best to help me understand that I would see Claire again. We sat—me, this calm woman, and her baby—until first light.

When I saw Claire walking toward me, she looked puzzled and sad. I flew to her side. She shook me and screamed to never, ever go anywhere without her. I nodded yes.

2

I have almost no photographs, no relics or mementos, to commemorate the gruesomeness and beauty of the days, months, and years Claire and I spent trying to survive. When we arrived in the United States, at O'Hare International Airport, we landed with nothing. The airline had lost our one suitcase. This had happened so many times: We'd lost everything. We'd been stripped, repeatedly, down to the skin.

That bag—big, black, soft-shelled—still haunts me. The suitcase was the product of so much struggle, and it contained everything Claire had worked so hard to provide: her kids' clothes, my favorite red sweater and my skirt with the buttons down the front, the plastic photo album Claire started in South Africa when Mariette, my niece, was a baby and we, very briefly, felt rich. Several photos in that album were of Mariette's birthdays, the date I used to measure time, as nobody celebrated my birthdays anymore. One photo in the album shows us at a water park in Durban, South Africa. Rob, the ex–CARE worker my sister married, is holding Mariette, and you can see fountains in the background, water droplets glinting in the sunlight. We look like a happy family.

The loss, the lights—the neon American colors overtook my senses, including my senses of reality and history, and the colors of Africa started to fade. My past receded, grew washed-out, jumbled, and distorted. I could no longer discern what was real and what was fake. Everything, including the present, seemed to be both too much and nothing at all. Time, once again, refused to move in an orderly fashion; the pages of the book lay scattered, unbound. This still happens to me: My life does not feel logical, sequential, or inevitable. There's no sense of action, reaction; no consequence, repercussion; no plot. It's just fragments, floating.

To make sense of my life, to reestablish a linear time line, I collect primary sources. I document myself. I collect and catalog detritus, junk: loose beads, old maps, stray toys, nice plastic bags, ticket stubs, buttons, paperbacks filled with marginalia. Often I travel with my *katundu,* my stuff: my pillow, my blue blanket, a candle to make the room smell like a home.

I wish I still had the mug my mother refused to let me take to my grandmother's house. In its place, I often look at the diamond heart necklace Mrs. Thomas gave me for my twenty-first birthday. It's an heirloom, the only one I have. Mrs. Thomas inherited it from her grandmother. When

Mrs. Thomas first fastened it around my neck, she cried and I felt loved and soothed by her crying. I thought to myself: *This is belonging. I'm not just a person who lives with somebody. I belong here.*

I keep, too, a gift my mother bought for me at her neighborhood Dollar Store for my twenty-fifth birthday: a small rectangular mirror pre-inscribed with a poem to a daughter. *I will always love you / For forever and a day / You're the meaning in my life / And precious you will stay.*

I keep photocopies of pages from other people's scrapbooks: images of me, wearing too-small borrowed clothes; me, standing next to the son of the American family who first hosted us. He's wearing, with no irony, a T-shirt that says I SURVIVED BASKETBALL CAMP. I keep museum handbooks, like the one I have on Rwandan basket weaving. I keep a My Little Pony that belonged to Claire's youngest daughter. I once put the toy in my bag by mistake when I was cleaning Claire's house.

My *katundu* is my ballast, exogenous memory, my solace, my hope. Some part of me believes that if I can just find the right arrangement of the pieces—if I can string all the beads in the right order, situate them in the right light—I can create a narrative of my life that looks beautiful to me and makes sense.

PEOPLE HOLDING "WELCOME TO AMERICA" signs were walking toward us. I was twelve. Claire was twenty-one. We stood erect and dazed as this bright white couple hugged the five of us: me, Claire, Rob, Mariette, age four, and Freddy, Claire's second child, age two. The couple had balloons for Mariette, Freddy, and me, the supposed children. They gave Claire and Rob $100 gift cards for Old Navy.

Claire and I had lived in seven different countries since leaving Rwanda. The United States was our eighth. I was callous and cynical. I didn't trust kindness; I believed it came with a price. I thought I could fool people into thinking that I was not profoundly bruised.

We just stared at our hosts—this middle-aged Germanic woman with short, curly blond hair and her skinny husband. They held a paper with our names. Their car smelled new. Their shampoo smelled like plumeria. There was so much concrete. I hadn't seen my mother in six years.

The moving car, my hands—it all felt weird and weightless, like we were still in the air, drifting, no obvious flight path. Just thirty hours before, we had been living in a slum in Zambia, one so poor that, when I returned to visit the place with Claire, seventeen years later, I jumped out of the taxi enraged.

My adult, credentialed, certifiably valuable self wanted to make the shoeless children there feel valuable too. So, against Claire's protest, I leapt from our air-conditioned cab into the heat and passed out a few sticks of gum from my purse.

This was a terrible idea. Claire knew it and I knew it too, though I'd blocked it from my mind. When those children's parents saw me, a wealthy-looking black stranger, giving their kids candy, they grabbed their children, scolded them, and marched them off, sure that my gift was the first move in a power play. I had been one of those kids, poor and living in that place, and I had never taken candy, not once. Candy was far too costly.

. . .

BUT NOW WE WERE HERE, in Chicago, with our balloons and the concrete. We were happy, or we knew we were supposed to be. We'd seen the movies. America the Gleaming.

Claire still had her smooth shiny skin, her wide smile, her eyes that look slightly more alive than everybody else's, her ability to bond with a stranger in thirty seconds, and her mirror talent of holding those close to her at bay.

She had heard Chicago was cold, so before we left Lusaka she'd bought us all puffy jackets. She had mastered the Zambian market. You could approach her in the morning and tell her you needed an ounce of gold, come back three hours later, and she'd have it done.

But now it was August in Illinois, steamy, and by the time Michele Becker, the short-haired Germanic woman, dropped all of us off at her pastor's house, on a leafy paved road in suburban Glenview, we were slick with sweat.

The pastor and his wife set up neat, comfortable beds for us in the basement—*you sleep here and you sleep here and there are the towels.* They covered their dining table with barbecued chicken, mushroom pizza, pepperoni pizza, salad, ribs, platters of fruit. Everyone was so nice, awash in a sense of purpose. But I was so bruised and so mistrustful of others that I didn't understand why.

I noticed that our new American sponsors hugged a lot. Claire and I didn't hug. I didn't hug Mariette or Freddy either, though I loved them and considered them my own and did everything in my power to keep them alive. Taking care of loved ones in my world was not based on affection. It was based on the fear of losing them.

. . .

WE LIVED WITH THE BEASLEY family, in suburban Glenview, for three months. Claire was pregnant again. Despite it all, she was a charming young pregnant wife, her hair tied in a knot on top of her head like a fluffy crown. Mariette was an innocent little girl. Freddy was a toddler. I was . . . what? A teenager.

The Beasleys had a daughter, Sarah, who was thirteen. She smiled at me and gave me a yellow bag with sunflowers on it and body lotion and wash inside. I used only a little bit at a time. I wanted it to last.

The Beckers, who first picked us up at the airport, had a daughter too, Julia, who was eleven. I didn't understand either her or Sarah. I didn't understand the way they laughed—they laughed at everything. They let their mothers do the chores. They spent their money on Smack lip balm. They talked to each other's parents so smoothly, with so few boundaries. Sarah said, "Hi, Michele!" to Julia's mother, no honorific. I could not connect.

Sarah had her own room. Both she and Julia wanted to make me comfortable, a thankless task. They planned a sleepover, then fluffed up the best pillow and gave it to me, and somehow that gesture, that fluffing, made them seem weak and silly in my eyes. I was so contemptuous, so defended, so easy to give to and difficult to please.

I could not relax. Claire could not relax. Neither of us had any ability to enjoy this plush new world. We'd worked so hard and run so far, only to go in a giant perverse circle. Now we were here. The Beasleys allowed us to do the dishes. That one chore, that was it. We were slipping, losing power in the unspoken economy, or so we thought. Claire made no money; she had always made money. Now Claire, with her too-alive eyes, watched cars go by.

In the middle of that first night in the pastor's house, when I woke to go to the bathroom, I climbed the stairs, opened the refrigerator, and stared. I'd seen huge refrigerators like this one only in magazines and on TV. I was amazed and impressed, and I could not stop thinking that if our neighbors in the slum in Zambia could see this, they'd be so appalled. How could one place have such excess while in another, just a plane ride away, people starved? Freddy had twiggy arms and a big round tummy from being malnourished. His body, here, now, would be fed and fixed. There were so many Freddys in this world.

My mind began toggling: *This is my life but this is not my life. I deserve this now because I suffered.* But then my mind ground to a halt. Had all the people who ate out of refrigerators like this suffered too?

EVERYBODY WANTED ME TO RELAX, to stop worrying about Claire's kids, to quit cleaning obsessively, to behave, at long last, like a child and start making up for all I'd lost. I was twelve years old but felt instead three years old and fifty years old, yet I knew I had to fit in. The other girls my age wore short shorts, so I wore short shorts too. But I could not be like them, languid and carefree. I had no feel for the concept of physical ease, not in any language. I raged with envy and anger and often I confused the two.

. . .

ONE DAY WHEN I WAS sitting on the lawn, watching cars go by, Mrs. Becker, who lived across the street, opened her garage. The space was dusty and overflowing with sports gear, folding chairs, lawn tools, paint cans, ladders, cardboard boxes.

I hauled everything out and placed it in the driveway, then swept the concrete floor, wiped down all the surfaces, restacked the boxes, and organized the gear. I found hooks on which to hang the ladders and chairs. The whole time Mrs. Becker kept saying, "Clemantine, *non*." I knew almost no English and not that much French, and could read only wealth in the detritus of their lives.

The kindness and gift-giving was overwhelming. Congregants at the Church of the Redeemer brought over secondhand clothes, books, toys for Claire's kids. Everybody wanted to help us. It made them feel good. I understand and respect that now, but I was only a few weeks out of the Zambia slum. Generosity was suspect and nothing made sense.

One day after breakfast, Mrs. Beasley drew a picture of a house on a piece of paper. Then she slid it across the kitchen table to me, along with a box of crayons, so that I could show her what my home in Rwanda had looked like.

I did not cooperate. I could not. I did not feel, not yet, that she knew what she was asking of me. I did not want to scratch back through my memory. I did not even really know how to access that once-safe place with the outdoor kitchen, the red roof, the birds-of-paradise. Nostalgia was a destructive exercise, a jab at a still-tender wound, stitched up poorly.

Claire and I talked about nothing, not ever. To say I

missed our childhood home would have felt perverse, like telling her that I missed wearing my baby shoes. Claire's lone concession to a yearned-for past was a desire to eat *ugali,* the thick cornmeal porridge we'd eaten so often in the past six years. *Ugali,* Claire told herself, was not memory but sustenance. *Ugali* was power: *We made a little money, okay, so we are not going to starve today.* Mrs. Beasley drove us into the city, to the World Market, which catered to Chicago's African and Latin American immigrants. The cassava and groundnut powder there seemed to make Claire, for a minute, feel whole.

Back in Glenview, Claire cooked her *ugali.* She stood at the stove with her belly and stirred. "If you don't eat *ugali,*" Claire said to me in Swahili when she served it, "you haven't eaten."

3

The farmers in Burundi must have complained. We needed too much. We now stole food and left nothing—we had nothing to give.

One day a Red Cross truck arrived. The authority felt reassuring. The driver of the truck invited pregnant women and the wounded to sit in the back. He told the rest of us to follow on foot. We were just a mass, a herd. We walked for almost a whole day before we arrived in Ngozi, at two hills covered with blue-and-white tents.

I joined the unhinged singing of names, wailing, "Pudi! PU-DI!," sure my brother would be here. Dozens of men worked as guards, and they corralled me back in line, next to Claire. These men only had to bark a few orders to establish their power. They looked just like us, but we were desperate, they were not. We did as told.

When we reached the front of the queue, a woman grabbed my hand and pushed it deep into a bucket of purple ink. The dye on my hand meant that I had been counted. Nobody asked my name—too many people for names. Nobody cared that I was six. Claire and I were given a tent, two water jugs, two scratchy blankets, a large plastic bag, and a pot.

A man pointed to the part of the hill where we should pitch our tent, then to the hollow between the two hills where we were to stand in line, once a month, to fill our plastic bag with maize and beans. The camp bathroom was located near the ditch that aid workers dug for dead bodies. I was afraid to go; Claire was not.

For a few hours I remained giddy. Of course we'd find our parents here. Then I looked around. Hundreds of sick on the ground, moaning. Dozens of wounded, yelling. Our tent was one in a square of twelve other tents. There was a stove, if you could call it that, in the middle. Squares of tents like ours—units—stretched out in every direction.

I LOST TRACK OF WHO I WAS. I'd become a negative, a receptacle of need. I was hungry, I was thirsty, I needed a bathroom, I needed a place to sleep. I was so confused. I just kept spinning. *How did I get here, where I am a nobody? We walked all this way, for this?*

Everywhere you looked you saw people turned to stone. If you touched them, they'd crumble to dust. So they remained still and silent, trying not to shatter. You cannot tell the story: *I lost my children, husband, my whole family—I have no idea where on earth I am.*

STAYING ALIVE WAS SO MUCH WORK. We had to wait five hours in line for maize and five hours again for beans. We had to fetch firewood. No one had matches, so just lighting a fire was a chore. You had to look out for smoke and when you saw some you walked over there, with some kindling, to carry the flames back to your unit.

You had to remember your unit number—not a given at age six.

You had to try to hang on to your name, though nobody cared about your name. You had to try to stay a person. You had to try not to become invisible. If you let go and fell back into the chaos you were gone, just a number in a unit, which also was a number. If you died, no one knew. If you got lost, no one knew. If you gave up and disintegrated inside, no one knew.

I started telling people, *I'm Clemantine, I'm Clemantine, I'm Clemantine! I don't want to be lost. I'm Clemantine!*

I thought if I stated my name enough times, my identity would fall back into place. I wrote my name in the dirt. I wrote my name in the dust. But a name is a cover, a placeholder, not the whole story. A name is a basin with a leak that you need to constantly fill up. If you don't, it drains and it's just there, a husk, dry and empty.

I lost myself anyway. Every little thing. I had always loved the fancy soaps at my aunts' houses. I loved the ones that smelled like geranium and lilac best of all. Now we had no toilet paper. Nobody in the camp had toilet paper. UNHCR, the UN Refugee Agency, had apparently decided that human dignity was expendable. There were too many of us to try.

I hunted for soft leaves—young iridescent eucalyptus. I smoothed them flat and kept them hidden in a corner of our tent. Everybody who had not given up entirely kept a secret stash. We all walked around with leaves in our pockets and did each other the courtesy of pretending not to see.

I FELT LICE CRAWLING DOWN my neck, out of my hair, toward my ears. I watched people sitting by their tents for hours, picking bugs out of the hems of their clothes. The lice in your clothes are smaller and harder to kill than the lice in your hair. I checked my seams—the waistband of my purple skirt, the cuffs of my red sweater. I found hundreds, maybe thousands, entire dystopic kingdoms.

When it was cold for a day or two, I forgot about the lice for a few moments. But when it was hot I was obsessed. Not even my body was mine. My hair was blitzed and occupied. My bed was blitzed and occupied. Same with my clothes. The eggs were everywhere. More were coming. They were coming. There was no winning.

So I surrendered. I sank back into the sea of degradation. Claire walked me over to a man in camp who had a razor, and he shaved my head. Almost all the kids in the camp were bald. I had not wanted to be like them. I wanted to be special. I cried for days.

Every surface, every body part, was a battleground in

the struggle to remain a person. I missed my mother most when I bathed. Claire wouldn't help me. I couldn't reach a spot on my back. Along with the lice on our heads, a whole other species of bugs burrowed into our feet. We waged a hopeless war against them. Our only possible strategy to win was impossible: keep our feet clean.

Claire found a big flat rock and placed it by our tent. Each morning we took turns standing on that rock and using the water left over from doing dishes the night before to scrub our feet. While still on the rock we put on our shoes. Then we spent the rest of the day trying to keep our feet from touching the larva-filled dirt. We failed, every day. How could we not fail? Our lives were structured for defeat. Our shoes were destroyed. We lived outdoors. Once the bugs had burrowed into your feet, you couldn't walk for days. You had to take a pin, if you could find one, and dig them out. If you couldn't reach them, or if you left a bug's head in your flesh by mistake, you had to soak your feet in ashes and salt water. If you could find any salt.

If the bugs remained, they multiplied. They tunneled to neighboring patches of skin. Once this happened, you spiked a fever. Good luck to the refugee who got sick.

THE MAIZE WAS GRAY, and hard as pebbles. It was nearly impossible to cook.

Our stove consisted of three cinder blocks with a clay cylinder built around them. You stuffed firewood in the holes inside. I was the lowest-ranking responsible person in our unit, so I was given an important, miserable job: watching the pot on the stove and adding water to the maize and wood to the fire, for four, six, eight hours on end. The stove put out so much smoke that I was scared I would go blind.

But I did not want to see anguished, angry eyes staring at me. I was vigilant and never once burned the food. We had no plates. We ate off the lids of the pots as platters. All the choices for how to consume the maize were bad. If you ate it right away, the maize burned your fingers. If you let it cool, the maize hurt your jaw to chew. It hardened completely, within fifteen minutes, as if it had never been cooked. The maize had no aroma and no flavor. I hated it and wanted to boycott meals. But if I didn't eat, my stomach growled all day.

I MADE A LIST OF things to cry about, so that if someone said, "Why are you crying?" I'd have something to say. *My stomach hurts, I had a bad dream, I miss my mother, that older boy is making fun of me.*

I did not usually know why I was crying. I did not know that I was not going back. Most of the people in the camp were poor farmers from southern Rwanda and Burundi. They knew they weren't going home soon. We were privileged—*abakire*. In Kigali, I had a TV. My father had cars. Here I had a sister who was indomitable, even if she resented me. Their fate was not mine.

People didn't like us very much. We were the rich girls, we had so much to learn. All the small luxuries of city life, the table manners, the cut flowers, Claire's dream of going to McGill—all that was useless.

We didn't want to tell people our parents weren't

around. When asked, Claire said, "They aren't currently with us right now." In response everyone said, *"Mana yanjye we!"*—my God, how poor, how heartbreaking! They looked not straight across but up and down on us.

When I was not cooking I sat on a rock and watched people coming into the camp, their faces slack with defeat and relief. I no longer had hope. I didn't expect to see my mother's hair, plush and wavy. I didn't expect to see Pudi's ropy arms. I could barely remember the rest of him.

But still I waited. I told other kids that if they sat with me while I waited I'd give them candy or balloons. The youngest of the children believed me. I felt no remorse.

WITHIN A MONTH, I HAD built a shellacked veneer, tough and thin. Each morning I walked two or three hours to fetch water. Then I waited in line at the pump, a plastic gallon jug in each hand, for an hour more. The other women, who were probably only seventeen, tried to bully me out of my spot.

"Are you going to be able to carry that jug? It's bigger than your head. It's bigger than your whole body."

I gave them my newly mastered do-not-fuck-with-me stare. I'd developed it by telling myself that I was twice as old and five times stronger than these pitiful women, who could only cope with their lives by making a six-year-old feel small. My act was not often well-received, nor was it always deployed well.

I took it upon myself to look after the other children at the camp, and they provoked in me contempt and rage. Many walked around naked. I considered them pathetic and weak. I had grown expert in one thing in my short life: I knew what it meant to be taken care of. Their treatment was not it.

One day UNHCR workers set out bags of clothes: old T-shirts, sweaters, underwear, pants. I grabbed an armful, took it back to my tent, and rounded up all the naked young children I could to give them something to wear. When I had run out of clothes I just yelled: "Where is your mother? Get out of here and go tell your mother to put clothes on you."

Parents complained to Claire: *Your younger sister is terrorizing our kids.* I could not help myself. I couldn't stand the naked two- and three-year-olds. They looked to me like strays—filthy, unloved, drooling, bugs crawling on their faces, flies around their eyes that nobody bothered to swat.

One day I tried to bathe a little boy on our rock. He lunged away, as if to flee, and I grabbed his wrist and yelled: "Sit down." Soon after, I started admonishing parents: "Put your kids on a leash!" Not long after that, I was forbidden to enter certain areas of camp.

I made a point of visiting the bathroom as seldom as possible. The biggest of my fears was falling into the disgusting pit latrine. One morning a child did. A man with a bucket had to fish him out.

WHEN WE HEARD THE WORLD FOOD PROGRAM trucks rumbling, all the kids would run, barefoot and shirtless, pushing and tripping each other on the uneven trails. The grown-ups didn't hurry. They dragged themselves, in their own time, over the hill with their torn plastic sacks. When asked, they flashed their red cards indicating their allotted portion of maize.

After a while we could barely eat it. The maize made people constipated for days. At night a young man from our unit snuck out of the camp and found a miller in town who could grind the maize into flour.

Flour! This made my life so much easier. I could now cook by stirring the flour in boiling water and letting that steep for fifteen minutes. Or I could add just enough water to make a thick paste, wrap the paste in banana leaves, and put the leaves over boiling water to steam. I could knead the flour and water into a dough and then cook that over dry heat, setting our pot on hot stones.

Someone, somewhere inside UNHCR cared just enough, or so it seemed to me, to realize that maize alone could not possibly sustain a growing body. So once a month aid workers called all the kids over to the Center for Children, which was really just a large tarp strung up to provide shade, with a dirt floor and no sides. We children were each given half of a red vitamin—half, not even a whole one.

Also once a month, on a different day, each child received a biscuit. The biscuits were made with soy and protein powder and they tasted like cardboard soaked in sugar.

Once a month: half a vitamin. Once a month: a biscuit. It was such horrible teasing.

I TRIED TO STAY VIGILANT about the bugs. I tried to stay clean. I tried to remember who I was *before*. I tried not to cry. But there were always bugs in my feet, and in my clothes, and in my bed. I worked at pretending that this was tolerable, that this did not make me feel repulsive, that this did not turn my world into a noxious yellow-green, that this did not make me feel buried, that this did not make me feel that I was worthless except as food. I succeeded in projecting this fantasy to others. When I polished up my armor I could project: *I am Clemantine. I am valuable. I am a fighter. I am human.*

But I could not fool myself.

The one tenderness I allowed myself was singing before I went to sleep. My mother taught me a song:

Scooch closer to God and tell him
Everything that is painful to your heart
Everything that makes you sad
Everything that makes you lonely . . .
Whisper to God
God has not forsaken you or abandoned you.

My mother taught me the song so I could cheer myself up when I felt wronged or was in a bad mood—say, if Pudi didn't want to play with me or I broke a favorite toy. I sang the song for ten minutes a night. I felt hurt all the time.

4

The night before I started school I lay awake rehearsing: "Good morning. It's fine to meet you. My name is Clemantine. Thank you."

We'd moved into a rented apartment on North Winthrop Avenue, on the north side of Chicago, near the Thorndale stop on the Red Line. One bedroom, on the fourth floor. It felt luxurious. The church had pooled money to buy us furnishings, so I now had a daybed in the living room, covered in a white spread and lots of pillows. Every time I walked into the apartment I thought, *This is my bed, my bed.*

I shared it with Mariette but I considered it mine.

My alarm went off at 5:00 a.m. I ironed my nice new American middle-school outfit, the jeans and sweater I'd picked out from Old Navy, and put on the choker Julia

Becker had given to me as a parting gift. By 6:00 a.m. I'd done my hair and brushed my teeth, and at 7:00 a.m. Claire walked me down the block to the Swift School. The George B. Swift Specialty School was three stories tall, with long banks of windows high above the street, and a square yard with a jungle gym. I noticed kids walking into the cafeteria to eat a free breakfast, so, good former refugee that I was, I walked into the cafeteria and ate the free breakfast too.

I was too old for any grade lower than sixth, so I was put in sixth grade. My teacher, Mrs. Garcia, wore lipstick and black square glasses and looked very fit. She kept mints on her desk. When she introduced me to the class, she pronounced my name exactly right.

I sat in the third row, near the windows. I spent the days drawing with paper and crayons. I had no idea what was going on.

ON SUNDAYS MARY ANNE, from the Church of the Redeemer, came to Claire's apartment to tutor me in English. She tucked her brown hair behind her ears. She looked as if she'd never been scared in her entire life.

Each week she brought a stack of notecards. On one side was a picture of a shoe or a car or a nose or whatever, and on the other side was the word SHOE or CAR. My job was to color the pictures. I found this very childish and soothing.

People asked me if I was happy. I was still unclear on what happy was. I drank chocolate milk at school at lunch each Friday. People from church threw a baby shower for

Claire and lavished her with onesies, a giant box of diapers, and a double stroller.

I was trying hard in my new role: to be grateful, to be teenager-ish. Yet I often felt overwhelmed and miserable and dreamed of jumping off the roof of the Swift School and floating away. The Beckers invited us for Thanksgiving and we were the most ridiculously stereotypical refugees. Claire whispered to me that she wanted to take all the extra food from the buffet and bring it home to sell it.

Christmas was the same: overload. A turkey and a ham. All the colors, all the smells, all the sounds made me dizzy. I'd grown alarmingly thin. I refused to eat and drink.

I could not believe any of it but I made myself believe it. I needed to see the world in front of me clearly to perform my part well. I needed to crack the code. So many times, in our former life, I'd had to become someone else in order to stay out of a refugee camp or out of jail, to stay alive. I had played a mother. I had played a yes-ma'am younger sister. I had made myself a nobody, invisible. Now I had become this strange creature: an American teenager.

Yet I wasn't like the teenagers at my school. My mother and father were . . . who? Nobody in my life attended parent-teacher conferences. Nobody made doctor's appointments for me. Nobody checked to see if I did my homework.

Eventually Mrs. Becker stepped in. Near the end of the year she talked to my teacher. I needed more—more resources, more guidance, a more stable home environment, one in which I could really be a kid. I needed to go to a better school.

. . .

THE WOMAN I CAME TO call my American mother was petite and blond, Southern and proper, and the only other thing I knew about her before she drove to my house to pick me up in her tan Mercedes was that she wore red turtlenecks and jewelry to church.

Mrs. Becker had spoken with Mrs. Beasley, the pastor's wife, who taught at a school called Christian Heritage Academy. Mrs. Beasley, in turn, convinced the school to admit me to repeat sixth grade. Christian Heritage Academy was in Northfield, the suburb next to Glenview, twenty miles north of the city and too far from our apartment in Edgewater for me to commute every day. To go to this school I needed a place to live, Monday to Friday.

That's where my new American mother, Mrs. Thomas, came in. Mrs. Thomas's older sons had left for college. She had empty rooms in her house in nearby Kenilworth. It was now late June. I was thirteen. I'd been in the United States a year.

Rob came outside and spoke with Mrs. Thomas, to make a show of confirming that the Thomases weren't inviting me to live at their house so that I could be a servant. I placed my navy backpack and small red tote bag in Mrs. Thomas's trunk. I brought with me only a few changes of clothes.

The air-conditioning was on. I felt so cold. Caulay, the Thomases' sixteen-year-old daughter, sat in the front passenger seat. No one had ever asked me if I wanted to move. I had never moved alone. In her lilting Southern drawl, Mrs. Thomas oriented me in my new landscape: *This is*

Lake Michigan. This is Northwestern. This is the beach where we swim.

We pulled up at a green-shingled house with a green lawn, a large porch in the front, and a detached garage in the back. Inside were green chairs and green carpets. Caulay took me up two flights of stairs to a large bedroom with two twin beds, a desk, several bookshelves, a radio, a box of cassette tapes, its own bathroom, and a peaked roof.

The Thomases had two dogs, Cotton and Ginger. They treated the dogs like people. This was a new experience for me. Dogs in Rwanda became a nightmare during the war. They started eating the dead.

I remember wanting to ask: *Is this all mine?* That first night I did not turn out the lights. I switched from one bed to the other and then remade the first. I looked through the cassettes and books.

This was a trial, for the summer. I would live with the Thomases and attend an art class at Christian Heritage Academy, and if that worked—which is to say, if I passed my test as a tolerable boarder—I would live with the Thomases and attend Christian Heritage Academy for the school year.

I didn't want to mess anything up. In the morning I made the second bed, replaced all the books and cassettes, dressed, and walked downstairs when I heard Caulay's footsteps. I ate cereal for breakfast because Caulay ate cereal for breakfast. Mrs. Thomas made me a peanut butter sandwich to take with me to art camp for lunch, and I told her I loved peanut butter and sandwiches even though I disliked them both.

My refugee skills were kicking in. I wanted to be who I needed to be and get what there was to get. There was a feedback loop that I could now see. If I performed well in my role as a student, people responded with happiness and pride and wanted to pour more resources into me. Fill me up again and again.

FOR MY FIRST DAY AT my new school, Sarah Beasley taped to my locker a big construction-paper star that said TINA. Mrs. Beasley had noticed that people often pronounced my name incorrectly—it's *Cleman-teen,* not *Cleman-tyne,* though everybody said the latter. So she decided that for school my name should be Tina. Tina would not be mispronounced. Tina would be much less cumbersome than Clemantine to shout if I played sports.

Afternoons, after I finished track practice or dance rehearsal, Mrs. Thomas picked me up, always in the same spot. She understood my fear of being lost or left behind. At home, I climbed the stairs and did my homework in my bedroom. I loved my space—the peace, the order. Everything was under my control.

Every weekend I returned from Kenilworth to Edgewater. Each time Mrs. Thomas dropped me off, I gave her a big smile, said, "Thank you!" and hurried out of the car before she reached over to hug me. Affection still made me flinch.

Claire's life was the opposite of mine: so many people, so much chaos. She now worked two hotel jobs, her marriage was unraveling, and she was raising three kids as a single mother. Her third child, Michele, was born American. That still sounds strange to me.

Friday to Sunday I cooked, cleaned, and took care of the kids. I didn't talk about my life in Kenilworth, and Claire didn't ask. She didn't know that my bedroom had two beds, or that under the stairs on the first floor of the Thomases' house was a bathroom with the most glorious red walls and a dish of soaps that looked like robin's eggs. She didn't know that I beamed with pride when Caulay introduced me as her sister.

WE SAID THE PLEDGE OF ALLEGIANCE. Then I went to first period in a classroom with large glass windows overlooking the playground. Soon after, everyone started panicking. The principal dismissed school for the day. Mrs. Thomas picked me up.

At home, on the TV, we watched the World Trade Center towers fall, again and again. Every five minutes Mrs. Thomas tried to call Brad, her older son, who lived in New York, and Mr. Thomas, who wasn't picking up his phone at his law office. She couldn't breathe. I felt nothing.

"This happens to people everywhere," I said to Mrs. Thomas many hours into her vigil. Horror flashed across her face. These were not the words of the nice poor African refugee girl she'd invited to live in her home.

I was awful: jaded and scornful. Why shut down the school? My nightmares returned. Every night I now dreamed of falling down the Thomases' laundry chute and landing in their basement, where I found myself trapped in a maze full of people with those faces I'd seen in Rwanda. I heard the noises of lives destroyed.

I could not comprehend why people were wearing American flag pins instead of packing their bags. I filled my backpack with extra shoes, a sweater, my Bible, a pencil case, and snack bars.

I clipped obituaries out of the *Chicago Tribune* and kept a list of the names of the dead. I resented and envied the acknowledgment. These dead were lucky enough to be memorialized and mourned. Here they were, named individually in the paper, each with a specific job, family, and hometown.

AROUND KENILWORTH, PEOPLE WANTED TO treat me like an egg, the poor fragile refugee girl. They said, with the best of intentions, "Let's do something special for you. Let's buy you something nice."

I was contemptuous and cold. My attitude was, *Okay, if that makes you feel better. If that's your way of giving, if it makes you sleep at night—yes, let's do something nice for me, fine.*

I was one of only three black students at my school. The lone black adult was the Eritrean janitor. When neighbors stared at me, Mrs. Thomas said, "Honey, just smile. You're beautiful."

People wanted to help in the ways they knew how to help. One day one of Mrs. Thomas's friends picked me up at school in her convertible, handed me a pair of sunglasses, and said, "We're going shopping today. Call me Auntie Wilma." Wilma Kline became my godmother of shopping. We drove to Marshall Field's. She'd clearly been there at least two hundred times.

"Clemantine, we need good boots for winter," she said, and then she walked me to the shoe department where several salesgirls knew her name. "Do you have those on sale? Do you know when they'll go on sale? Do you have the Ralph Lauren collection?"

She knew every inch of every floor of that department store. She was a superhero of sorts to me. I recognized in her the ability to navigate an overwhelming space with complete mastery and confidence. For years, both Claire's life and mine had depended on just that skill: reading a complicated, unfamiliar space; judging who would be your friends, who would be your enemies, how do you navigate with ease, how do you survive, how do you escape?

I still ask myself those questions all the time. If something happens, where would I go? Who is strong in this situation? That person is trying way too hard—why? This person is extremely friendly—does he want something? Money? Favors?

"Okay, here's how it works," Mrs. Kline said. "You buy things you can mix with things you already have. It's not only about trend but what will last longer."

After the boots we tried on clothes, outfits that would work for school and outfits for the weekends.

Mrs. Kline wanted to teach me about my body, help me find comfort in it. Maintaining my body had been so much work, so costly. Protecting it had been a never-ending battle. It was not a source of joy. I had been dragging it around for thirteen years, trying to keep it from harm. I felt like it stood in my way.

At Marshall Field's, Mrs. Kline pulled a red polka-dot dress off the rack and said, "This is an investment piece."

Then she collected an armful of white blouses, tank tops, shorts, jackets, jeans—everything—and took me back into the hushed private dressing rooms to try them on. Mrs. Kline had opinions. She instructed me to try on the jeans first with one blouse, then another. Then try the jacket with the boots. Some looks she liked, others not.

"You don't want to look like a hoochie mama," she explained, rejecting low-rise jeans.

I did not fully understand her project at the time. I did not know how much I was broadcasting my pain, how obvious it was to Mrs. Kline that I needed help loving myself. I thought I was more worldly than this godmother of shopping. So I tried on the clothes thinking, uncharitably, *This is nice but why should I care.*

BUT THE TRUTH IS, I needed Mrs. Kline. I needed the confidence and positivity she wanted to instill in me. Claire never talked to me about my body. I knew the basics of how my insides worked from eavesdropping. When we'd been on the run, we'd seen girls on their period, trailing blood. But there was no discussion or celebration, just taboo and fear.

I struggle to this day. I don't know if I want to have children. In Rwanda, if you're female, you are born with great value—not because of who you are as an individual or your mind, but because of your body. Because of your body, when you marry, your family will get cows. Because of your body, when you marry, your family will get land. Even for a city girl in Kigali, this holds true. Yet at any moment the value of your body can be stolen.

You can be ruined—*konona,* that's the Kinyarwanda word for rape. I knew the word *konona* by the time I was four years old. My mother didn't say it, but I heard it around the neighborhood. A young girl would go out to play and her mother would yell after her:

"Don't be ruined. Don't let your life be destroyed."

The word itself does such violence. Because once you're ruined, that's it, that's what the word tells you. The damage is permanent. You have no value and you will never get it back. The evil that was done to your body is now intrinsic to your being. The clear water of your body is poisoned. You are hostage to that idea.

I work every day now to erase that language of ruin, to destroy it and replace it with language of my own. With *konona,* you're told, there is no antidote, no cleansing agent. Your family won't get the cows. Your family won't get the land. You're polluted, you're worthless—that's it.

My body is destroyed and my body is sacred. I will not live in that story of ruin and shame.

MRS. KLINE BOUGHT ME MY eighth-grade graduation dress. I loved how she saw me by then—she saw beyond me, into a beautiful future. The dress was black satin, strapless, with sky-blue panels on the sides. "This is a dress you can wear forever," she said.

She took me shopping for sandals to wear with it. She knew my body well, as well as anybody then, my narrow wrists, my skinny feet. When she told the salesgirl my size, she asked her to bring pads to keep my feet from sliding around.

I considered my feet a vulnerability. They resembled my father's feet: dark, narrow, small nails, with veins that looked like tree roots when I stood. For so long I'd been telling myself: *My feet are too ugly and shameful to show the world. Animals lived in them. My feet reveal that I am weak.*

I hadn't told Mrs. Kline that narrative. I still kept that story to myself. The salesgirl kept bringing boxes—strappy sandals, wedge sandals, slingbacks. I tried them on and stared.

Mrs. Kline and the salesgirl favored a patent leather pair with an ankle strap and just one band across my instep.

I tried to see my feet in the mirror as someone else's feet, and I decided they were good.

WINNING, IN KENILWORTH, WAS CHEERY. You smiled, you got the best grades, you collected the most friends, you performed the highest cheerleading jumps.

I kept my fierce self hidden. Life was easier that way. The only time she emerged was with Susan, a girl in my grade, a bully who was pretty enough to get away with it.

Early in the year Susan decided to have a pool party, and one day she walked around the lunchroom, table by table, inviting all the girls except Jane, who was sitting next to me. Jane's family was from Eastern Europe; she was petite and quiet, an easy target.

Later that afternoon, when we lined up for gym class—teachers at Christian Heritage Academy made us line up for everything; we were all to be obedient servants of God—Susan happened to be in the bathroom, so I excused myself from the line, entered the girls' room, and locked the door. Susan was at the sink, washing her hands. When she finished, she started in on her hand sanitizer, her chapstick, and all the lotions in her purse.

I just stood, close to the sinks, and then said, "Hi, Susan."

I did not use my nice Kenilworth middle-school voice but instead my do-not-fuck-with-me voice, which I hadn't realized was so close to the surface. I didn't want to get kicked out of the Thomases' house or expelled from school, so I'd buried that fierce persona.

Susan opened her mouth to speak, but I cut her off.

"If you're ever mean to Jane again, you'll pay for it. Just because I'm being nice and playing nice and choosing not to play your mean-girl games does not give you the right to go around and bully people."

Susan's pink skin turned bright red. The voice that came out of my mouth was untamed, instinctive, aggressive, a hawk defending the hummingbirds on her turf from nasty blue and gray jays. Susan repacked her lotions into her purse and yanked on the door handle to leave, but the deadbolt was locked.

I enjoyed watching her fear more than I expected, more than I wanted to admit.

I unlatched the door and walked out.

I JOINED THE CHEERLEADING SQUAD. I'd seen the Christian Heritage Academy cheerleaders stretching in the gym. They looked so happy, all bubbly, with matching peppy smiles and blue-and-white skirts. I had never considered just smiling and being happy. It seemed like a useful skill. I wanted to do that.

The physical challenge suited me. It took me out of my brain. If I closed my eyes and paused I saw magma and mayhem. So every free moment, I practiced. In the shower I performed the moves in my mind. I wasn't used to the American rhythms, but I liked forcing my body to move as I willed it to. I liked the control.

Girls invited me to Old Orchard Mall. They invited me to McDonald's for milkshakes and laughed when I complained they were too sweet. They invited me to sleepovers, but after attending two I stopped going. All night the girls would talk about who liked which boys, who were best friends. They wanted to share secrets and bond.

I did not want to bond. It was easy to perform the rituals of casual friendship, but this I didn't want. These girls who believed they were my peers were not my peers at all. I thought: *We can have this moment, but we will never be best friends. I've seen this before. This is just how it starts: all cute and adorable and they're buying you soda and candy and the next thing you know, they want to kill you.*

5

Claire taught me never to accept gifts. She learned this from our mother. There are no gifts, Claire said. No candy, no bread, especially from men. She insisted on figuring out how to survive indebted to no one, so she hustled.

UNHCR forbade refugees to leave the camp. But Claire noticed people near the edge of the camp trading with the Burundians who lived nearby. The locals had almost nothing themselves. They lived like the family who'd taken us into their hut. They wanted to trade for the cheap plastic containers UNHCR gave us to carry water. They wanted to trade for the soy powder UNHCR gave us so we would have protein.

This lit Claire up. Anything we couldn't use she brought to the fence. "Do you want this?" she asked, showing a man's sweater to a sixteen-year-old boy. "This is very nice. This will look very nice on you. I'll take that bag of potatoes."

One day, near our tent, I noticed Claire singing. One of the camp managers was Canadian and had the power to give a few refugees jobs. Claire knew that to get a job, here, at her age, in this sea of ruin, she had to broadcast her scrappiness, intelligence, and drive. So she practiced the only English song she knew, "Home Again," over and over. *Home again! Home again! When shall I see my . . . Home again! Home again! I shall see you when I return . . . Home again!*

She had no idea what the words meant. Neither did I. But she belted out her song for the camp manager as if this situation was not totally perverse. Claire would not hand over her dignity. She would not let you believe that you'd hollowed her out. She did not say her name out loud, like I did, chirping like an idiot, protesting too much. Claire said her name to herself. But she understood that to have a life she wanted, to hold on to her identity, she did not need you to see her in a certain light; she needed to retain that light from within. Beyond that, she needed money. She needed a job.

The camp manager heard Claire out. Then he asked, "What useful skills do you have at your age?" Claire said she could help take care of the orphans at the camp, organize volleyball and basketball games for them, create clubs like the Boy Scouts and Girl Scouts, lead them in dances and songs.

Claire got the job. She coached the girls in sports and pulled them to the side and said don't take candy or bread from men. I didn't join.

. . .

I DID OUR LAUNDRY IN the river. This meant leaving camp midmorning, so I could be there at noon. Upriver was for drinking, downriver for washing.

Along the shores stood giant boulders and large pine trees, odd envoys of permanence in a crumbling world. To wash clothes, as I learned from watching the older women, you first make a ring of rocks in the river. You soak your clothes, along with smashed pine needles, inside that ring. Then you pound each clothing item against a rock to shake loose the filth and bugs.

On really hot days, while the clothes soaked, I swam and watched the heat rise off the hills. In the distance, the valleys looked like water. I wanted to play. I wanted to be back in the mango tree with Pudi, pretending that we were on a bus to Butare. I asked the older women, "Can you see it? Can you see the ocean?" They had no energy for my games.

Around 1:00 p.m., I wrung out our clothes and laid them on the hot boulders. By early afternoon, the stones had absorbed so much heat that our wet skirts, T-shirts, and underwear sizzled when I spread them out. The hope was that the heat of the rocks would burn the lice and nits. This worked, sometimes, with thin cotton but never with the blankets, into which the nits burrowed too deep for the rocks to sear. To delouse the blankets you had to boil them in a gigantic pot.

At night, I listened to people talking around the fire at our unit. The banter was raunchy, a release for the adults, but the laughter and stories unmoored me. I yearned to be protected, and I was not protected. Each night, I floated away, half asleep, half awake.

In my dreams, I walked around the camp collecting all the stuff I could find, everybody's forks, beds, pots, and chairs, all the belongings anybody had left. I carried that stuff back to my tent and I built an enormous pile, a fantastical tower of junk, all the clothes, water jugs, stacks of stoves. Once I'd built the tower, I climbed up to heaven to look for my parents. I didn't want to have to die to find them. I wanted to see them but remain alive, tell them that I was okay. So I built my rickety spire, climbed, and looked around. In those dreams I got close to my parents, I knew they were there, but I never actually saw them. I never even asked God where they were.

IN KIGALI MY MOTHER HAD insisted that we check in on our elderly neighbors. Claire insisted on that now.

There was one old couple in our unit—maybe eighty, very short, with black feet. They never wore shoes. They were Batwa, members of one of Rwanda's indigenous tribes. The woman, who I called *Mucyechuru,* or Grandmother, wore an orange cape and wrapped a cloth around her head. She argued with her husband about his cooking. I'd never seen a woman stand up to a man like that.

Her husband, who I called *Musaza,* or Grandfather, spit when he talked. He had a tattered brown hat with a wide brim, like a cowboy hat. His eyes were sunken, his teeth were terrible, and the curly hairs on his chin were gray. On Sunday he wore black pants and a white shirt, and he used a rope as a belt.

I adored them. I began lingering at their tent to avoid going to the bathroom. I still had a horror of slipping and falling into the feces and was scared of catching a disease. So I'd stand there, hopping around, asking Mucyechuru and Musaza to tell me stories so I could distract myself from needing to pee. I so craved a narrative, especially now that nothing made sense.

Musaza told me a folktale about a giant clay pot that never broke, no matter how hard people tried. Rocks, lightning, hammers—nothing could shatter it. The pot contained enough soup to feed the world. I wanted to find it. I learned how not to pee for a really long time.

Mucyechuru and Musaza had always lived without much. When God passed out gifts, they told me, God gave some people land. He gave others height. When God got to the Batwa people, he had nothing specific left, so he told them to share the forest.

ONE DAY MUCYECHURU AND MUSAZA invited me to join them foraging in the woods. They looked for amaranth leaves to make the maize tolerable to eat without oil.

We walked on faint paths up the hills into the pine trees. The forest floor was covered with pine needles and clover, and Musaza scolded me if I stepped on the clover. "If you treat the plants with disrespect," he said, "they become angry, and angry plants taste terrible."

Buried in the ground cover we found mushrooms—Musaza called them the meat of the forest. In the brush we found green tomatoes—a miracle to me; I hadn't seen a tomato in months.

Mucyechuru and Musaza moved their hands and feet with a gentleness that made me ache, the gentleness of Mukamana buttoning my bathrobe. When they found a tomato plant, they placed a few pine boughs around the stalk and leaves to hide the treasure.

Nobody in my world was tender and protective of me anymore. Certainly not Claire. Claire refused to stand in line to collect only two scoops of maize when we were meant to be given four. What did it mean that Mucyechuru and Musaza were protecting the tomatoes for the future? Would I still be here?

Of course we were starving, so Mucyechuru and Musaza taught me to eat bugs: grasshoppers, the green ones. The black grasshoppers, Musaza said, were trying hard to stay alive. The green ones we could eat as long as they were flying toward us. This meant the grasshoppers were grateful to have been alive and ready to give themselves up as food.

We also foraged on people's farms. This was stealing, yes, but Mucyechuru and Musaza stole with a code. When you pick someone's vegetables, Mucyechuru told me, you have to leave something to grow back—clip a vine and tuck it into the soil or plant a seed.

NEAR CHRISTMAS, CLAIRE WOKE UP with dysentery. I'd already seen it a dozen times. Someone wakes up with a fever. Throws up. Their bowels explode. They scream and scream until they're too weak to scream. They shit blood. By night all the water has drained from their body and they've lost seven pounds.

Many children in camp who got dysentery died. Their

small bodies, already so malnourished, could not withstand such a brutal attack. Many adults died too. The cycle was always the same: scream, vomit, shit, bleed, then get rolled up in a bedsheet and placed by the latrine to be buried or burned.

The morning Claire woke glassy-eyed and delirious with pain, I ran to find Musaza and Mucyechuru. They moved Claire's bed—a palette of grass—close to the door of our tent, so that she could have fresh air. Musaza made her drink a potion made of charcoal and a bright green tincture of leaves. Claire still screamed and vomited and shit blood. All day I prayed, if you could call it that. Really I just pleaded: *Please don't let her die.* There was no alternative, no room for *what if . . . ?* Claire had to make it. I was seven.

For three days Claire moaned and drifted in and out of consciousness. I slept outside with Mucyechuru and watched the moon. It was the only time I slept away from Claire.

At last her fever broke. I found some charcoal and mixed it with water and leaves and tried to make Claire drink it. She refused.

NOW I FEARED THE LATRINE even more. For hours I'd stand outside Musaza and Mucyechuru's tent, asking for stories.

Musaza told me about a girl who thought she was the most beautiful child in the world, and how her stepmother tricked her and told the child to sit on a mat, but the mat was covering a giant hole in the earth and the girl fell deep inside. The girl tried to climb out but failed. She screamed and no one came.

He told me about the moment when the sun goes down

on the shore of the ocean—that's when you can lift up the sea and walk underneath and visit wherever you want.

He told me that if you hike in the moonlight you can enter *Tera,* the landscape of the past.

"Are there animals there?" I asked.

"Yes," Musaza said, "of course."

"What type of animals?"

"What kind do you think?"

"Lions? Are there lions?" I asked.

"Yes! Beautiful lions, so grand and big and they don't hurt anyone."

"Are there tigers?"

"Yes, majestic tigers, so fast and smooth you can ride on their backs."

"What do the lions and tigers eat?"

"They eat vegetables," Musaza said, "just like us."

"Where do they sleep?"

"They sleep on the ground and protect us."

The plants, the animals, the ocean, the people—everything in Tera was alive and just as I wished. Musaza outlined a world for me and allowed me to fill in the colors, gold, silver, copper, and brown.

I turned around and lectured the other children. "Hey, do you want to know what Musaza told me today? He told me that a long time ago you just could just call crocodiles and they would come and you could lie on them."

AFTER WE'D BEEN AT THE camp for a couple months, a handsome Zairean CARE worker declared that he was in love with Claire. She was, somehow, as magnetic as ever, her dark eyes undefeated and alight. Rob was twenty-five and seemed extremely sophisticated and put-together, with his well-cut hair, clean crisp jeans, striped shirts, and shiny shoes.

Claire told Rob that she was too young to get involved, that the last thing she needed was to be a sixteen-year-old refugee without any parents and with a little sister and a baby to care for. But he persisted.

"Me, I want to marry you," Rob said daily. "Me, I want to marry you. You can go to school."

"You see me in this camp suffering? You think I'd be better off pregnant?"

Still, every day, Rob tracked down Claire and told her that he'd fallen in love with her the day we entered the camp. He promised her that if she married him, we could move to Zaire and live with his mother.

Claire knew we were targets, two girls without a guardian. Every woman was a target there. Our lives were impossible, hopeless. One woman in camp cried all day, every day. People screamed at her: "You don't think we all want to cry? We all want to cry." We all knew very little separated her from us.

That's life in a refugee camp: You're not moving toward anything. You're just in a horrible groove. You learn skills that you wish you did not know: how to make a fire, how to cook maize, how to do laundry in the river and burn the lice on the rocks. You wait, hoping the trucks will bring something other than corn and beans.

But nothing gets better. There is no path for improvement—no effort you can make, nothing you can do, and nothing anybody else can do for you either, short of the killers in your country laying down their arms and stopping their war so that you can move home.

The only way out was marriage. Marriage came with papers. This made Rob, with his handsome smile, an escape hatch, a ticket out. When Claire finished work, she saw Rob, in his clean clothes, in the camp office. Every time he asked her, "Do you want to go back to school?" *School.* Now, instead of looping in a circle of terrors, Claire's mind had a place to go, a destination far away from the faces she, too, wished she'd never seen and the screams she, too, wished she'd never heard.

And once Claire had possibility, so did I. I did not understand why we had to remain in this nightmare because we lacked papers, but I accepted that it was true. Besides, I had Claire to look after me, and Claire had no one to look after her, and she refused to believe that this, here in Burundi, was the life she deserved. Bugs, filth, hunger, death. Claire said yes to Rob.

Claire and Rob married, at camp, surrounded by a few envious refugees and a couple of Rob's friends and coworkers. I wore my favorite green skirt. The best things about the day were the sweet fried *mandazi* and sodas.

ROB DID MAKE GOOD ON his promise. After the wedding, he took Claire to Bujumbura, the capital of Burundi, to get official marriage papers. The plan, from there, was for Claire to continue on to meet Rob's family in Zaire, in the city of Uvira, and for Rob to come back to the camp to collect me.

So Claire was gone, and now Rob was gone too, for

three days. I spent each one of my hours alone, terrified, my stomach aching. I told myself if neither Claire nor Rob returned I'd walk back to Rwanda. I didn't talk to anybody. I worried that if I did speak I'd slip up and reveal our plans, and people would turn cruel with jealousy. Then Rob did return. He found me in front of our tent, in silence, and I felt scared to leave.

We'd been in Ngozi a year. Earthy, mystical Musaza and Mucyechuru were now the only people in my world besides Claire. We left them everything we had, but I didn't say goodbye to them. I just put on my best clothes—my green skirt and white blouse that washed easily and dried quickly in the sun—and I bundled up my few possessions: a couple of sweaters, a smooth rock I'd found by the river, the flip-flops I'd repaired with string, a few toys I was told were gifts from children in Canada.

Rob walked me over to his CARE truck. Inside, on the seat, were two plastic bags, one with a new dress and colorful sandals, another filled with treats. I was not polite. I stuffed *mandazi* and candy in my mouth, and drank Fanta, all at once. I did not say thank you. I felt sick.

The road was long and bumpy. I threw up. I was exhausted, so much more exhausted than I realized, and I fell into a deep, hard sleep. When I woke I panicked. I didn't know where I was. I could not find my way back to camp.

If I could not find my way back to camp, I could not retrace my steps to Butare and then to Kigali and get home. I knew I was supposed to feel relieved, but I felt despairing. I didn't want to look out the window. Loss is loss is loss. I did not want to see more miles streaming by. I didn't want to pass more stacks of hills.

. . .

IN THE EVENING WE ARRIVED in the city. Bujumbura looked lighter and smaller than Kigali. Rob drove us to the home of some friends who lived on the outskirts of town, in a big compound. The gate squeaked loudly when Rob opened it.

Inside, in the courtyard, sat a large family—grand-parents, cousins, aunts. I locked eyes with a woman who was about Claire's age. She was beautiful, with a wide smile, white teeth, and black gums, and such excellent posture and shiny hair that I could tell she'd had a good life. She walked over and hugged me, and I cried.

She called out for the other children. Four or five came running, then stood close, grabbing my hand, acting like we were friends. I felt so numb, dissociated. I'd forgotten about casual warmth. I'd even forgotten about implicit trust. The young woman with the excellent posture brought me a cup of warm tea, sweet and rich with milk.

Pleasure. I could barely remember how to enjoy plea-sure. For a year I'd been so consumed with survival—though not that, really. I was consumed with something much smaller and more banal: making it through the day. *Let's get through today,* that was my mindset. *Then it will be tomorrow. Let's make tomorrow happen too.*

The young woman disappeared again and came back with a bowl of rice-flour beignets. The grease stuck to my hands. She asked if she could bathe me. I refused.

The following day she took me to the market. It was hot and dry, hotter than any day at camp. On the way we saw a naked man walking down the road. Nobody tried to stop him or heckle him. They just let him keep walking, as though he were a legitimate part of their world.

The young woman with excellent posture bought me a yellow dress with white lace ruffles on the back. I'd wanted a ruffled dress like that since I was four. I thought the dress looked like an ornate rice dish that Muslims served at the end of Ramadan. She also bought me four pairs of underwear. It had been a year since I'd worn underwear without a broken elastic waist.

WE STAYED WITH THE FRIENDS for two days. Then Rob and I took a bus west, to Uvira, on the shore of Lake Tanganyika, to meet Claire. En route, I fell asleep, and when I woke we were in a valley. The sun was so strong. Some trees were plush, canopied, and rubbery, and there were palm trees and cacti too. We were ordered out of the bus to pass through a border check. The wind was hot. Dust filled my eyes and mouth. An officer read Rob's papers and glanced at mine. He let us pass.

Back on the bus I willed myself to stay awake. I stared at the faces of the people walking on the road, the kids playing soccer, the large houses, the vendors selling oranges, fish, candy, bread. I wanted it all. I scanned the landscape and tried to commit it to memory so I'd know how to return. We passed beautiful houses, gardens with pink, purple, and white bougainvillea flowers.

Eventually we stopped at a vast blue body of water. I thought it was a river or the ocean—I'd never seen the ocean—but Rob said it was the lake. The water was a dark luminescent blue. I could not wait for sunset. At sunset I could lift up the water and wave it like a carpet and visit all the creatures in the universe underneath.

From the lake we hitched a ride on a motorcycle up a hill, to Rob's uncle's house—a long red-brick single-story building with glass windows in front, wood shutters on the sides, and a tin roof. Claire was inside, in a long embroidered pink-and-yellow dress. I found that completely disorienting, too, as she'd only ever worn tomboy-style clothes before.

The house smelled like garlic and onions. Rob's five cousins, ranging in age from five to seventeen, wandered around, bright and clear, a whole intact world. Rob's mother and aunt were preparing big plates of rice, eggplant, and fish stew.

I ran to the couch and cried. I wanted to go back, but I did not know where. Nobody talked about home.

The boys shared one room and the girls another, so I slept in a room with Mwasiti, who was eleven years old, and Dina, who was fourteen, all of us in one bed, me in the middle, because I was scared.

Claire, because she was now married, had a room on the far other end of the house, with Rob. For my first few weeks I constantly stood on our mattress and tried to touch the ceiling. We'd been sleeping outside for a year and a half.

I TRIED TO IMPERSONATE A regular child, the child I had been or had wanted to be—loose-limbed, relaxed, playing Kick the Can, running through the streets and in and out of people's homes. I tried to imagine what Pudi would do. He was

confident, fun, slightly rebellious. I was self-conscious and
didn't fit in.

Over the previous year I'd learned how to pass the hours
with detached lethargy because all there is to do at a refugee
camp is kill time. Now I watched Mwasiti scrub pots after
lunch. She worked with furious efficiency. In two minutes
the densest, greasiest smoke residue disappeared and the pot
looked new. Mwasiti and Dina laughed at my pace with
sweet, protective affection, like I was a baby bird with a
broken wing, their sad, tender project, hobbling around.

I cried for days, maybe weeks. Then I pulled myself together. I returned to asking the only question in my life:
How do I survive here?

Rob's family, like everyone else in Uvira, spoke a mix
of Swahili, Kibembe, and French, and each morning at
five Rob's aunt, Mama Dina, woke up to pray, loudly. Her
prayers were nothing like my mother's rehearsed Catholic
prayer. Sometimes Mama Dina invoked angels. Sometimes
she chastised evil spirits. Mama Dina didn't only address
Jesus or Mary. She didn't say anything by rote. She spoke
to God directly.

"God, it's just you and me. What is happening?" she
said, mostly in Swahili. Sometimes she called him Dad, as in
"Dad, we have kids who are hungry, people who are tired.
You've always taken care of us. Keep us healthy. Shield us
from evil. Bring an end to this war. We have no medicine.
Help us here."

Rob's father had disappeared, and Mama Dina's husband returned only on occasion, but she never complained.
Whenever Mama Dina cooked or spoke or moved, she did
so with a fantastic physicality, her hair pulled back tight

against her scalp. If she asked you to do something, you obeyed. She was my news service. I learned what was going on in the world through her prayers.

Of course we woke up the moment she started praying, but we lay in bed listening and did not get out of bed until six.

ROB'S MOTHER, WHO WE CALLED Mama Nepele, was slighter, with lighter skin, high cheekbones, and a far gentler, more subtle presence. She wrapped her tight curls up in a cloth and she held my hand when she spoke.

Once I could make it through the day without weeping, she enrolled me in second grade. She altered some of Mwasiti's old royal-blue uniforms to fit me. On the first day I was so excited to be going to school again, but it turned out to be a stern, punitive Christian academy with instruction in Swahili and French.

I knew almost no Swahili and only a few French words—*maison, voiture*—and anytime I mispronounced vocabulary a nun walked over and whipped the back of my hand. If a student was late, a hand got whipped. If a student talked back, a hand got whipped again. After just three days, I tried to persuade Mama Nepele to let me quit school. She sat me down next to her, held my hand, and refused.

To sweeten the deal, Rob, with money from his CARE job, bought me two pairs of sneakers—one blue with yellow laces, the other Velcro Nikes. Claire found the cutest uniform for me, a royal-blue jumper with overall-like shoulder straps that crossed in the back. Still, I didn't want to go to school.

For breakfast each morning we ate fresh bread, purchased from a man who walked by the house with loaves, and drank chai tea with milk and sugar. I didn't like the chai but pretended that I did. I dipped my braided bread in it, and once the bread started disintegrating and my mug was filled with crumbs I declared it too messed-up to drink. At which point Mwasiti said, "Let me help you with that," and drank my chai herself.

Afternoons, once the nuns released us, we ran home and played marbles and roamed the streets. As I began to relax, Mwasiti and Dina introduced me to the dozen women that they called Auntie, all of whom swept me into their care. My hair was now growing out. It was thick and wild.

Every day some auntie would say, "What is this mess?" and then sit me down to wash and braid it. I felt so special. Everyone was special. *You have the longest hair, you have the shortest hair, yours is the thickest.*

Women gave me freshly ironed Sunday dresses that their daughters had outgrown. They offered to cut my nails and paint them, to scrub my feet. Throughout they listened to the radio and boasted about the food they would cook—the bone marrow, the beans. They bragged, with affection, about the produce they bought. *Want to know what I got at the market? I got these fresh onions and the garlic. Did you get the garlic? Oh, you didn't? I'll show you. Look how beautiful it is.*

Because Uvira was on the lake, the whole town ate fish from Monday through Thursday. A lot of times at the market people would say, *I have too many fish, take some.* The kids even sang silly songs about it: *Don't be so stingy. There's enough fish in the lake to dry, to fry, to roast.*

. . .

THE WEEKENDS WERE A PARTY. Beef, chicken, elaborate sauces, pounded cassava leaves cooked in palm oil with garlic and nuts—plus the most fabulous clothes. Zairean women and men dressed. I'd never seen anything like it, an elaborate mix of European and African styles—French- and Italian-looking blouses, Chanel-style coats, head wraps from Senegal, secondhand clothes imported from France, Spain, and the United States.

In Rwanda, dressing up meant looking respectful, proper, and tidy. Clothes were meant to hide you. A good Catholic kept her body uncelebrated, under wraps.

But Zaire wasn't overwhelmingly Catholic—it was also Muslim and Protestant, Middle Eastern, African, Indian, and European, a vibrant mash-up. Clothes were costumes, a means of self-expression, buoyant claims to beauty. Claire loved it. One day she wore a long, brightly patterned dress, the next a tailored blouse and skirt. The women dressed for one another, partly to prove that their husbands, fathers, and brothers were providing well for them. Claire started a business, selling purses. They were so beautiful.

On Friday afternoons, men stood in long lines at barber shops. Women packed salons, some panicking if their hair was not yet washed and blown out as the sun was going down. On Saturday and Sunday, the men wore suits and ties. The streets were filled with music, radios cranked up in living rooms and front doorways.

When a new song came on, the adults paid children to dance. I didn't know how, and I was shy, so I stood back, behind Mama Nepele if possible, and I watched. Then I practiced when no one was looking.

BEFORE LONG I STARTED TO forget. I started to forget the camp and forget Rwanda. Most nights we ate together as a family, ten or twelve of us, including an unmarried uncle who often came for lunch and stayed through supper. Mama Nepele began hinting that if he was going to eat at the house every day, he ought to bring along some fish.

We all sat around a shared pot of sweet-potato-and-greens stew, beans, or roasted sardines. If you were slow—and I was slow—you missed out. So Mama Nepele started setting aside a plate just for me, a small serving tucked away in the kitchen. I loved her for it. I felt embraced, remembered. She always spoke to me softly and patted my hand, and I relaxed.

I learned more Swahili too. Words in Swahili are like a dance. When I'm angry, I think in Swahili because that's the language in which I learned to fully express my emotions.

Early mornings, in the dark, I giggled with Mwasiti and Dina in bed during Mama Dina's long crazy prayers. On weekends we pulled the TV outside on the front porch and danced together in the big front yard, eight or ten kids, trying to match all the dance moves in Papa Wemba music videos.

One night, I had a very strange dream. It was about a black cat with earrings that turned into a person. A few days later a woman came over. I thought she was the cat lady. No one liked her and I didn't know why. I mentioned my dream and this woman to Claire, and she said talking like that would get people in trouble. Rwandans take the dream world seriously. When you wake up, people ask, "What did you dream about last night?" It's like saying good morning.

Maybe this life, here in Zaire, was my real life and before was just a dream.

CLAIRE FELT TRAPPED. SHE WANTED to go to school, as Rob had promised, but she couldn't because she was now pregnant. So she bided her time in Rob's family's house, telling me that someday soon we would be going home.

I could tell she was lying. She didn't know, and I knew she didn't know, and I resented her for it. No one had phones. No one even talked about reaching my parents—it was impossible. None of my shoes from Rwanda fit. I'd lost so many teeth and I hated the new ones that had replaced them.

Claire spent her days dressing up—kitenge dresses, chic European knockoffs. What else was there for her to do? Rob left for two or three weeks at a time, to work at the camp. His was a good job, and he was a good son and dutiful husband. When he returned to Uvira he brought gifts: fancy lotions for his mother, beauty products for Claire, matching Nigerian World Cup soccer T-shirts for all the kids, each one in its own plastic tube, which we all treasured and saved. He shared his salary with the extended family and he bought a little plot of land, high on the hill, with a view of the lake, on which he planned to build a house for Claire, himself, the baby, and me.

As Claire's belly grew, all of Uvira started calling her

dada, the Swahili word for sister. That terrified me. Our grandma had told us: *You lose your language and you disappear.* Claire could not lose her name.

For Christmas, just after I turned eight, one of Claire's friends gave me a Mickey and Minnie Mouse backpack. It was bright pink with orange shoulder straps and an orange belt that fastened at the waist with a satisfying snap. Minnie wore a red-and-white polka-dot dress, and both Mickey and Minnie had enormous white shoes. I adored it.

Mama Nepele had a purse that was full of treasures: lotion, pens, a small Bible. Inside the backpack I kept the rock I'd saved from the refugee camp and my favorite marbles, to show to Pudi someday.

A FEW MONTHS LATER, IN March, Claire, then seventeen, checked into the hospital in downtown Uvira, like a regular pregnant person, a member of the community, and gave birth to Mariette. With that she became a minor celebrity, our young queen. People brought Claire food, *kanga,* comfortable slippers, jewelry, anything she wished for.

After school I hung around, waiting for leftovers. Some days, Mama Nepele ran a clinic for me and the other girls, teaching us how to hold up Mariette's head, how to change a diaper, how to give her a bath, how to keep her warm or cool. I thought Mariette's belly-button cord was revolting and sneered in disgust. Mama Nepele picked up my hand and said, "That's how the baby was connected to the mother."

"Where does it go?" I asked. "The part that connects?"

"That's a different conversation," she said.

Still, I fell in love. Mariette was a doll, *my* doll. I didn't want any of the kids besides me to touch her. I obsessed over keeping her clean.

Claire was less possessive, less bossy. She loved Mariette, but she did not seem to want this life.

WE WALKED DOWN THE HILL to the lake to swim. Past the mango trees, the guava trees, the fish market, the beautiful houses on the water. On the way the kids all teased each other. "If you want to braid Clemantine's hair, you better clear out the whole month! Her hair is like a forest!"

I had no idea how to tease back—my mother punished me if I so much as told Pudi that he had a big head—but I recognized the affection. We swam all morning, until our skin looked ashy and wrinkled. Then we filled buckets with water and powdered Omo soap, washed our clothes, and sunbathed on the sand until they dried.

Mama Nepele usually gave us some money and someone would run to the market to buy cassava bread and roasted fish for lunch. I never wanted to go home, back up the hill.

Two more cousins, Mado and Patrick, arrived when Mariette was four months old. They came without their parents on a boat from the south, carrying big bags of red palm oil, dried fish, and yuca bread. Their family was having a hard time keeping them out of trouble and feeding them, though it was not an emergency yet.

Mado, who was my age, was still a little chubby. Patrick, who was five, still felt entitled to be babied. He was constantly complaining, in his charming way, that he was too hot or too cold or too little to do chores. He demanded that we sing to him; only Mado would.

Some nights the electricity was cut off—those were my favorites. One was especially dark, midnight blue with black shadows, and all the kids in the neighborhood came to our house to play Kick the Can, because we had the biggest yard. Among them was Serge, a boy from school with dark black skin on whom I had a huge crush. All day at school I doodled his name on my notebook. He drew pictures of flowers on scraps of paper for me, but we never spoke.

That night moved with delicious slowness. We played for hours.

Long into it, when all our limbs, even our eyelids, were slack from exhaustion, Serge got tagged and ended up in our Kick the Can jail, where several other kids were already confined. A few moments after that I heard my name called. I'd been spotted and needed to avoid getting tagged or I'd end up in jail too. I ran faster than I'd ever run before, reaching the can and kicking it over—a great victory.

Serge and his fellow prisoners were free! They lifted me up, like a soccer star who'd scored the winning goal. Serge smiled and said, "Next time I want you on my team."

People there were so kind. There's a lovely word in Swahili: *nishauri*. It means "advise me." When someone was mad at you, they would come to your house and sit down and talk and say, *This is very disrespectful and I think we should consult each other on how to move forward. Let's make peace here and come to a conclusion that is beautiful.*

. . .

THE SPELL BROKE A FEW months later. People began streaming into Uvira, knocking on doors, begging for meals. Zaire had been the pride of Central Africa for breaking free of Belgian and French control. But now fighting was breaking out to the north.

Soldiers were starving their fellow countrymen by cutting off food supplies—that's about as much as I understood. Mama Dina and Mama Nepele cooked extra fish stew and rice, and desperate strangers came to eat.

People kept coming, stumbling off buses, flooding the markets, emptying the shelves. Mama Dina prayed with zero filter. "God, protect the kids with guns. Bring them peace. Clear their minds. God, take care of the hungry."

Soon we didn't have enough food for our family. Men stopped fishing. It felt too dangerous. We ate one meal a day. School closed down. The police imposed a curfew. The electricity and water were cut. Just as in Kigali, the world pulled inward.

Mama Dina's prayers grew louder and more intense. "God, give common sense to the people throwing bombs. Bring medicine to the sick and dying. God, whup those who are doing evil. God, shield our house."

Police and soldiers lined the lakefront. In the evenings, you could hear the shooting.

"God, this is your house. It will not be shaken by any storm. Not a storm made by men."

CLAIRE DID NOT WANT TO wait for more trouble. So Rob arranged for us to take a boat to a town close to Kazimia, where some of his extended family lived. Claire gathered her jewelry and clothes, anything she could sell. She told me to stuff my clothes in my backpack. We needed to leave.

This was not a joint decision or even a real discussion: *I think we should leave. How do you feel about that?* It was a command: *We're going, now.*

The boat took us to the western shore of Lake Tanganyika near the Lukuga River, a lush equatorial paradise. It was gorgeous and I hated it at first sight. When we arrived at the wharf, the soldiers shouted, "Twenty dollars, twenty dollars, twenty dollars." Claire gave them money. "Document, document," they said. Claire showed them our bogus papers. They let us pass.

Rob's uncle was a pastor, well-respected for converting his whole village to Christianity. Everybody was lovely to us—so much so that soon some people grew skeptical and began to gossip. What was so special about us? But inside the pastor's compound, just as in Uvira, all the women wanted to braid my hair. They wanted to pull me under their wing. They wanted to cook for me and teach me how to pound cassava. I didn't want the affection. I was finished calling new people Auntie. I couldn't do it over again.

I now felt I'd made a mistake in Uvira. I'd let my guard down. I'd allowed myself to feel I belonged. But there was no real belonging—not anymore. There was only coming and going and coming and going and dying. There was no point in letting anybody get close.

As I walked around the village, people would say, "How was your tea this morning? How is your family? I see you are buying three loaves of bread. Do you have visitors? Where are you from?" To this last question I had no answer.

So I tightened my focus on Mariette. She was my big

Barbie, happy, smiling, oblivious. Claire often took off during the day; I didn't know where she went. Maybe she resented all the roles and rules—*be a wife this way, be a mother this way*—that the local women wanted to impose on her. I assigned myself the role of Mariette's eight-year-old mother. I carried her everywhere. I fed her whenever she made the slightest noise. I stared at her while she napped.

Sometimes Rob's cousin, who had three kids of her own, would insist on caring for Mariette. She thought she was being nice, but I felt threatened and displaced. She tied Mariette to her back with a cloth. She took Mariette down to the lake to bathe. She walked and sang until Mariette fell asleep. I hated her for it—hated her casual competence. She was stocky and strong, and she yelled at her children when they misbehaved. I didn't have anyone to yell at me.

I missed Pudi more than ever, his stinking Adidas shirt. I felt him slipping away in my mind. I remembered the Tintin adventures, slicking up the patio with soap, watching him climb the more fragile trees. I saw his dark ropy arms. That was it. I felt so deeply alone.

I never expected Claire to coddle me. Even before we ran, we'd had terrible fights. When I was five I stole her white watch. I snuck it into my bag to show the other children at school, but even after my mother punished me for taking it, I could not find the watch. Claire never forgave me.

Now she was my life and she was gone. I changed Mariette's diaper fifteen times a day. I wanted her bottom to be dry, very dry. I worried we didn't have enough powder. I didn't want Mariette to get a rash. Mariette could not get sick. She had to stay clean, impeccably clean. I allowed almost no one to touch her. When Claire returned at the end of the day, I asked, "Have you washed your hands?" before I allowed her to nurse.

Eventually Mama Nepele arrived. I cried with relief.

But by then Kazimia was shutting down. The electricity and water had been cut off and replaced with terror.

FLEEING KAZIMIA REQUIRED NOT JUST traveling along the shore of Lake Tanganyika, but crossing it, a six-hour trip. Fifty frantic people, including one of Rob's cousins, crammed with us into a small boat. We carried our whole lives—or what we still had left of those lives. Rob's cousin had lost a baby a few months before. Malaria, no medicine. A natural disaster with a war assist.

We started taking on water as soon as we left. The only way to slow our sinking was to make our boat lighter, to trade possessions for lives. So people began dropping heirlooms—framed pictures, silver, jewelry—into the water and watching them disappear.

The looks on people's faces, the look of panic. It's easier to scream. But we'd all been trained not to scream, because if you scream you'll get shot and what's the point if everyone is screaming with their faces already? One woman tossed her china plates, one by one; then she started on glass teacups.

Still the cold water kept rising, creeping up the adults' shins, over my knees.

I prayed like my mother prayed, to every saint that I could remember—Mary, Rose, Catherine. Then I prayed like Mama Dina and promised God that if we made it to the other side he could kill me any way he wanted. I just didn't want Mariette or any of the kids on the boat to die like this.

I promised if we got out, I would be the best child ever, the best sister. I would be so good and kind and generous—I just didn't want to die in the water. There's no trail you can leave in the water.

I told God I would die anywhere but here. I prayed for hours and hours. The whole boat was quiet and I was sobbing and praying and I did it for so long that I don't think I could say anything more.

The water was a monster. Claire held Mariette, then seven months old, up to her chest. I wanted to hold Mariette but I was too short. I could not bear to think that she could die. Life was easier, emotionally, when it was just me and Claire.

Now we had this other life, sinking into this terrible maw. The moon was full. I willed myself to be light as air, to atomize and scatter in the wind. Water crept up to my waist. I lost my voice. No one said a word.

6

My eighth-grade English teacher at Christian Heritage Academy put the word *genocide* on a vocabulary list. I hated it immediately.

I did not understand the point of the word *genocide* then. I resent and revile it now. The word is tidy and efficient. It holds no true emotion. It is impersonal when it needs to be intimate, cool and sterile when it needs to be gruesome. The word is hollow, true but disingenuous, a performance, the worst kind of lie.

It cannot do justice—it is not meant to do justice—to the thing it describes.

The word *genocide* cannot tell you, cannot make you feel, the way I felt in Rwanda. The way I felt in Burundi. The way I wished to be invisible because I knew someone wanted me dead at a point in my life when I did not yet understand what death was.

The word *genocide* cannot tell you how I felt when my mother refused to let me take my clay mug from our home in Kigali to my grandmother's house in Butare. The word *genocide* cannot explain why I still think about that moment, why I still miss that mug, how I wonder if my mother didn't let me take the mug because she knew the true, intimate danger, because she knew who I was—who we were—at that moment would be destroyed, and thus she wanted to retain a piece of innocent six-year-old me.

The word *genocide* cannot articulate the one-person experience—the real experience of each of the millions it purports to describe. The experience of the child playing dead in a pool of his father's blood. The experience of a mother forever wailing on her knees.

The word *genocide* cannot explain the never-ending pain, even if you live.

The word *genocide* cannot help the civilians. It can only help the politician sitting in the UN discussing with all the other politicians in suits, *How are we going to fix this problem? These people have committed such horrible crimes. They've suffered such horrible things. They need water, they need food, and oh . . . wait . . .* Their attention drifts, time to move on.

The word *genocide* is clinical, overly general, bloodless, and dehumanizing.

"Oh, it's like the Holocaust?" people would say to me—say to me still.

To this day I do not know how to respond and be polite. *No,* I want to scream, *it's not like the Holocaust. Or the kill-*

ing fields in Cambodia. Or ethnic cleansing in Bosnia. There's no catchall term that proves you understand.

There's no label to peel and stick that absolves you, shows you've done your duty, you've completed the moral project of remembering. This—Rwanda, my life—is a different, specific, personal tragedy, just as each of those horrors was a different, specific, personal tragedy, and inside all those tidily labeled boxes are 6 million, or 1.7 million, or 100,000, or 100 billion lives destroyed.

You cannot line up the atrocities like a matching set.

You cannot bear witness with a single word.

I STARTED READING ELIE WIESEL'S *Night* that April. I was sixteen. The book alarmed and comforted me. I wanted to consume it whole. The main character was not a curiosity, not a member of that strange category—"martyr." Wiesel was white, European, male, and Jewish. Wiesel was me.

He expressed thoughts I was ashamed to think, truths I was afraid to acknowledge. He described walking in the snow—the cold, the mouthfuls of bread and the spoonfuls of snow, an injured frozen foot that felt like it was no longer his, "a wheel fallen off a car. Never mind." I had walked in the heat but it was the same walk—desperate, disembodied, surreal. I couldn't stop staring at the page. I needed to study every detail, and every detail humiliated me. The way he talked about his father, the devotion and resentment. That was Claire.

I did not yet know the political history of Rwanda. I knew the president's plane had been shot down—I remembered that now. My mother, terrified, came into my room early one morning and told me he was killed, and then we knelt down and prayed. But that was it. I just thought of the enemy, then, as bad guys who steal. I believed they were going to steal us, but worse. I thought, *Abajura* . . . People are coming.

Then they did come and I ran away from the bad people and the bad people stole my parents from me.

In the intervening years I had no references. Nothing to order or anchor my thoughts, and for a time I stopped trying to discipline them or pin them down. I didn't ask questions. Nobody wanted me to ask questions. I had a cousin who sometimes slept at Claire's house and he woke up from his nightmares screaming. But it seemed better to be like Claire. Claire was numb. She focused on building a life here, now, not excavating and examining in the Midwestern American sunshine the secrets that nobody wanted to see.

I had been shut down so many times. By my mother, my father, my sister. Everyone, every time I asked, said, "You talk too much." *Checkeka*.

I had a few floating fragments of memory, bits of seaweed in a fish tank. I remembered my mom folding things and putting things away in a way my mother did not fold things and put things away.

I remembered my grandmother burying objects in the ground, objects that nobody buried, and I remembered that when she saw me staring she shooed me inside.

I had been so absorbed, as a young child, in knowing the world, and then I'd lost the whole world that I knew. In the years that followed I wanted to piece that world back together, but the idea of one group of people killing another group of people—people they lived with, people they knew—that chunk of knowledge could never fit itself in my mind. It was categorically, dimensionally, fundamentally wrong. It was like trying to store a tornado in a chest of drawers. That was not how the universe worked.

Now I was sitting here, in Kenilworth, across a rift in the galaxy a million miles wide, learning about one group of people killing another group of people, people that they lived with and knew. This genocide, I read in very matter-of-fact terms, started on April 8, 1994, and lasted one hundred days. One group, the Hutus, killed another group, the Tutsis.

A radical fascist Hutu political movement called Hutu Power used the radio to spread its vile, cynical propaganda: the Tutsis were subhuman insects. *The cockroaches—* inyenzi—*have no right to live here,* they said. *The cockroaches' wealth is creating your poverty. The cockroaches are using their cunning and charm to steal and defile your women. They cannot be allowed to exist.* The fascists would not tolerate anyone standing by, refusing to participate.

Everybody, all Hutus, must join the cause of killing the cockroaches, and raping cockroach women, and if a Hutu doesn't perform his or her duty that Hutu will be killed or raped too. The leaders prepared for this savagery for years. They stockpiled weapons. They claimed killing cockroaches was necessary, a legitimate, honorable act of self-defense.

Just thinking about the radio, the physical object in my parents' living room, felt cataclysmic. The radio just sat there, spewing hate.

I tried to read Philip Gourevitch's *We Wish to Inform*

You That Tomorrow We Will Be Killed with Our Families. The book is a meticulously reported account of what happened in Rwanda in 1994: the killers calmly working down their lists of victims; the massacres in churches; the intentional gruesomeness of Hutu Power leaders arming everyone with machetes—they wanted the Tutsi murders to be painful and grotesque. The Nazi death camps were too tidy for them. I filled up the first 135 pages with little blue and pink stickies. Then I couldn't go on. The book's cover photo shows an empty chair at the edge of a lake. If you know nothing, the water looks serene. Once you understand even a little bit, you know the apocalypse is underneath.

Still I kept seeking information, digging up and deflecting facts. Almost eighty years before the genocide, the Belgians colonized Rwanda and infected the country with their cruel, bogus science of eugenics. Before that, Rwandans lived together in relative peace. Then the Belgians racialized the country. They measured people's noses and skulls. They created and consulted pigmentation charts, dividing the citizens into Tutsis, Hutus, and Twas. The Hutus made up the overwhelming majority, about 84 percent of the population; the Tutsis were 15 percent, the Twas 1 percent.

Then, three ethnicities established, the Belgians issued identity cards. Next they created social policy and propaganda campaigns designed to cause the races to antagonize each other, channeling Rwandan citizens' hatred onto one another other and away from them. The Tutsis, the Belgians said, were more like Europeans. They deserved respect, power, education, and cattle. The Hutus, on the other hand, were stupid, childish, dirty, and lazy. The Belgians barely bothered themselves with the Twas.

The Belgians left Rwanda in 1961 and 1962, but the poisonous thinking had taken root. And in the intervening years we'd done something so horrible that we couldn't even talk about it. The rest of the world fled Rwanda in its darkest hour and must live with that moral stain. On April 8, 1994, the day after the Rwandan president's plane was shot down, ten Belgian soldiers who had remained in Rwanda to protect the prime minister were brought to an army base and shot, beaten, or hacked to death. And that was it. Ten lives, and UN peacekeepers left Rwanda. The international community left Rwanda. What was going on in the country was too ghastly, too crude, too dangerous. All those countries that ended World War II by saying *never again* turned their backs. We Africans could kill each other if we wanted. We were not anybody else's problem.

Now, these many years later, I was in school in Kenilworth and the killers were being put on trial in hundreds and thousands of village tribunals called *gacaca* courts, as Rwanda's existing judicial system could not possibly try so many cases. The goal was to convict and sentence as well as heal, in the manner of South Africa's Truth and Reconciliation Commission, somehow to make it okay for you to coexist with the neighbors' family who killed your family, with the neighbors' sons, father, and brothers who raped your daughters, mothers, sisters, and wives. The facts about *gacaca* were reported, with alternating horror and equanimity, in the *Chicago Tribune*. In Kenilworth everyone read the articles and then looked at me, sad and alarmed, waiting for me to react.

My thoughts and senses became jumbled again. I felt dizzy. I felt hot. Time melted and oozed, then re-formed and solidified misshapen. The *Chicago Tribune* said 800,000 people. I could not begin to comprehend what that number meant as a number of people killed. My scale of reference was just so different. That could not be a number of people murdered. My teachers wanted to help. They invited me to ask questions about anything. I felt so tired.

I READ *NIGHT* IN BED. It transfixed me. Mrs. Thomas called me to dinner but I told her I was sick and couldn't eat.

Wiesel packed in so much, so efficiently. He loses his name. He loses all sense of himself. The depravity of his tormentors makes him depraved. "Bread, soup—these were my whole life. I was a body. Perhaps less than that even: a starved stomach."

I was fascinated, perhaps most of all, by his willingness to question the existence of God. No one in my life did that. Not my mother, not Claire. The only book that either of them ever read anymore was the Bible. Even in Kigali, my mother kept a shrine of saints and none of them had skin that looked like hers. The Thomases, the Beckers, the Beasleys, they did not question God either. They praised him daily. They never doubted his wisdom. Yet how could God exist?

Wiesel had the only possible answer: God was cruel. "Where is He?" Wiesel writes. "Here He is—He is hanging here on this gallows. . . . Praised be Thy Holy Name, Thou Who hast chosen us to be butchered here at Thine altar."

I could not absorb the book and I could not put it down. Wiesel was—I was—nothing, reduced to nothing, and yet still contained a galaxy of horrors. "I was dragging with me this skeletal body which weighed so much."

"The days were like nights, and the nights left dregs of their darkness in our souls."

Wiesel's father falls ill with dysentery, just as Claire did. Wiesel's father dies in the bunk above him at Buchenwald, and Wiesel feels nothing but relief—relief at being released from the burden of love in such a blackened world. "I did not weep, and it pained me that I could not weep. But I had no more tears. And, in the depths of my being, in the recesses of my weakened conscience, could I have searched for it, I might perhaps have found something like—free at last!"

I FINISHED *NIGHT* IN TWO DAYS. The following afternoon, during a free period, I sat on the classroom couch of my English teacher, Mrs. Ledbetter, and waited.

"This is exactly what happened to us," I said when she entered the room. "The walking. Everything. Strip, strip, strip, then you're nobody."

I showed Mrs. Ledbetter my copy of *Night*. I had underlined or highlighted ten sentences or phrases on each page.

I read the book a second, then a third time, to make sure I wasn't crazy. I listened to the book on tape. I was fascinated by Wiesel's determination to view himself without pity, shame, or sentimentality, to spell out the horrors he lived through and place himself in the fallen world.

I had no language to describe the atrocities of my life— not then. I think I barely do now. But after reading *Night* I remembered people in Kigali calling each other snakes and cockroaches.

I remembered people walking with luggage on their heads. People dropping their belongings on the side of the road and collapsing beside them. Panicked voices mixed with silence. People asking, "Did you see him?" Children crying, "Where's my mom?"

I remembered people snickering, dismantling each other. *Look how they walk. Look at their little legs. Look at their wide hips.* I'd learned a one-word label for the war, or conflict, or whatever it was: *intambara*. That was the hook on which I tried, for years, to hang all this in my mind. Just that one slippery hook. It was not enough. There is never just one word.

I NEEDED OFFICIAL IDENTIFICATION. The entire eighth grade was flying to Washington, DC, to learn about the Civil and Vietnam Wars, and to join my classmates I needed documents. I was sixteen, with no birth certificate and no passport. Claire and I had tried twice to get IDs. We'd stood in line at the DMV to apply for Illinois State ID cards, but each time, when we reached the counter, a clerk glanced at our tattered I-94 immigration forms and pushed them back to us, saying, "Next."

But without an ID I couldn't go. The state did not recognize me as a full person, with equal freedoms and rights. Mr. Thomas decided to get involved.

As a rule, Mrs. Thomas provided my care, the deluxe suburban middle-school package: the endless driving to and from school, the laundry, the meals, the lessons, the check-ins, and the thousand other kindnesses I absorbed every day. Mrs. Thomas made it her mission to take away my pain, at least the pain I displayed to the world. If I was sick, she brought me soup and saltines. If someone looked at us funny, she said, in her drawl, "She's my other daughter, my African daughter."

Mr. Thomas was a lawyer. This was his department. So one Saturday morning he woke me at 6:00 a.m. and we drove to the secretary of state's office, where Illinois issues driver's licenses. He planned to try his luck as an upstanding white American. Other than my I-94, the only official-seeming paper with my name was an exit visa from Burundi, undoubtedly fake. We arrived at the office and waited. At 7:30 a.m., when it opened, we received a number.

An hour later I stood at the counter, silent, while Mr. Thomas talked. "This young lady is from Rwanda," he said, launching into my story. "When she was six she got out the back door just in time to not be killed in the genocide. She lived in refugee camps for six years before settling in Chicago and living in our home. She has an opportunity to go Washington, DC, with her eighth-grade class. I think the state of Illinois would want to be supportive of her going to Washington to learn about our democracy and continue on her upward path. She's come twice before to get an ID and been unsuccessful."

The clerk behind the counter looked up. Mr. Thomas appeared to be such a perfect citizen, tall, clean-shaven, and distinguished. "Sir, what papers does she have?" the clerk asked him.

Mr. Thomas slid her my I-94 and my Burundi visa and

the clerk looked them over, bewildered. But Mr. Thomas's story grabbed her just enough not to reject us outright. She told us to wait for her supervisor. We lined up again a few booths over.

Ten minutes later Mr. Thomas started once more. "This young lady is from Rwanda. When she was six she got out the back door just in time . . ." Mr. Thomas was now practiced at his great American tale. He finished and stood silent, leaving it to the manager to weigh his perfect looks against my imperfect appearance, and to weigh her allegiance to humanity against standard procedure.

"Interesting story," the manager said, and then she smiled. "Good luck, young lady. Take this slip and return to the photo line downstairs."

This left me with a crucial decision: how to spell my last name. In Rwanda my baptismal name had been Uwamariya. The *U* at the start meant "I am of" Wamariya. But on my exit visa my name was spelled *Wamariya,* with no *U* attached. Wamariya had been my name in my American schools.

Claire's last name was different: Mukundente. It means, *How much do I love?*

As far as I knew, my last name was mine and mine alone. Mr. Thomas's mindset was practical, as always. "This is the moment to change back, if you think you'll want to. It'll be much more difficult later."

I stuck with Wamariya.

I STOOD ON THE BATTLEFIELD at Antietam and listened to the guide say that 23,000 people died, were wounded, or went missing there in a single day. Twenty-three thousand people. In one day. In a civil war. There was no blood anywhere. No women crying because their children had been killed. No grandmothers burned. The spring grass looked so fresh, so gentle. The field had once been stained red.

The next day we visited the Vietnam Veterans Memorial—all those names, each for a soldier destroyed. I'd been living in my armor, trying to maintain a fantasy that I now inhabited a better world. I lived in a country that told itself that it did not have wars at home. Now I broke down. So many named young dead men on that Vietnam memorial. No memorials or walls dedicated to dead Vietnamese civilians. I ached with jealousy for those named. I walked around the low black monument, sobbing. A teacher tried to comfort me but I still couldn't stand to be hugged. She encouraged me to return to the hotel but I didn't want to.

Meanwhile, my classmates took pictures. They were so lucky. They did not identify with the dead.

AT THE HOLOCAUST MEMORIAL MUSEUM, a docent handed me an identity card.

On it was a picture of a bald German man with round glasses—Jacob Unger, a salesman. He was gassed in the Sobibór extermination camp in 1943. Before that, he had a wife named Erna and two children, Max and Dora. He taught Hebrew in the evenings. The Unger family fled to the Netherlands, as refugees, in 1938. Five years later Jacob and his wife were sent to Westerbork, a Dutch labor camp. A week later he was sent to Sobibór, in Poland. He was seventy-two years old.

Later that semester, in Chicago, a Holocaust survivor came to speak to our class. She showed us the number tattooed on her arm. I envied that she had a language for talking about what had been done to her, a way of describing and ordering a world that had tried to reduce her to nothing.

Claire maintained order in her world by believing that God had a plan. Other Rwandans we knew in America partied too much, or drank too much, or watched endless Nigerian soap operas. They shut out the reality of the 800,000, the fact that members of their families and friends had been killed by other members of their families and other friends. They attempted to blot out the past and push on with their lives.

No one I knew acknowledged, as Elie Wiesel and other Holocaust survivors did, *Yes, this happened. Yes, people destroy each other. Yes, it is intolerable and turns you into a corpse. But still you must remember and you must carry on.*

IN 2004, WHEN THE MOVIE *Hotel Rwanda* came out, a student in my class asked me if I had been scared during the war. He was the first peer to ask me that question directly. I took offense. *You want me to tell you how I felt? How dare you ask me to return to that place.*

Soon the questions grew worse. People wanted to know if anyone in my family had been murdered, and if I had seen people get killed. I could not believe their sense of entitlement. These people did not have the right to my pain. They did not even realize that they wanted it, that they saw my life as a movie. Their questions felt prurient, violating, evidence of their inability to see me as fully human.

I understand fear of and fascination with death are central to the human condition, but I didn't want to be asked about death. I did not want to be a tool or a case study. I did not want to be that Rwandan girl.

Yet inevitably I was a curiosity, an emissary from suffering's far edge. People asked me to speak at church youth groups. They asked me to speak at Catholic charities. The requests came through Mrs. Thomas, who declined most of them for me. The events broke me down.

I did agree to speak to a class at New Trier High School, since it was the high school I'd be attending the following year. "Just talk about your childhood," the teacher said. I wasn't ready to do that. I felt scared and out of control at the idea of sharing my interior life.

So when I walked into the classroom of half-interested freshmen I asked the teacher to pull down the wall map of Africa. That way I could stick to the itinerary. My character would be unimportant. "I was born here," I began, pointing to Rwanda. The country looked to me like a gallstone in the center of the African body, a ball of pain. "We had a wonderful life and all of a sudden everything started to change."

I narrated my life as an adventure. *I learned to speak seven languages. I wandered across a continent.* I told a true story, though one that conveyed nearly nothing.

In return, the class reacted without pity, which was the point. They just thought I was cool. I hadn't known that was possible—that I could gain social status if I told my story in the right way.

When I finished, one of the students asked, "Did you have any animals? Like did you have elephants?"

I tried to spin the query into what seemed like a cultural exchange, asking, "Why do you have those metal things on your teeth?"

Another girl called out: "You didn't shower for days? Gross!"

I pretended I didn't hear.

So few people knew who I was. Often adults said to me, "You're so strong, you're so brave." But I didn't want to be strong, I didn't want to be brave. I wanted a fresh, fluffy brain, one that was not tormented by wars and fear. I wanted to backtrack in time to a world of innocence, to regress into the landscape of *The Boxcar Children*. It was so nice there. The children did not have parents but it was okay. They went places together. The brothers and sisters took care of one another.

My life, at present, felt like a tar pit. I felt like I was disappearing, being consumed. My story was just so interesting—so foreign, so exotic. It was *The Jungle Book*.

"Oh my gosh, do you know Clemantine?" people said. "I know Clemantine. She's a refugee. She's African. I think she had to pass through some forest or she almost died on some lake."

7

We reached Tanzania catatonic and exhausted. The boat pulled right up to the beach. Steep hills rose just twenty feet from the water's edge, so we fell asleep on the sand. It was so cold. Our whole boat had nothing. Rob's cousin who'd come with us now had nothing. She'd left Zaire with one bag. In that bag was her whole remaining life—all her money, her husband's college diploma. It disappeared overnight, while she slept.

The next morning, immigration police rounded us up and we resumed being refugees.

We spent one night at a nearby school, on a classroom floor. I wrapped Mariette in our one blanket, yellow with white flowers. Then I put her inside our one remaining suitcase to keep warm. I worried constantly about Mariette catching cold. I was nine. I knew babies died from pneumonia. I could not allow her to die.

All night, in the yellow blanket, in the suitcase, Mariette remained silent. All the children with us in the school had stopped crying. Only the adults wept. Rob's cousin wept. The next day we rode one of those godforsaken white UNHCR trucks to a refugee camp in Kigoma.

You could tell from far away that people wanted to get out of the camp. Police were stationed all around the fence. We felt like cattle. Rwandans. Zairians. Burundians. It didn't matter to our keepers. Nobody had a tent. You just picked a patch of dirt. Claire didn't speak. We didn't eat for two days.

There were not enough bathrooms. The latrine lines took hours, too long to wait. People relieved themselves everywhere. Hundreds of people lay in the red dirt, sick.

I scanned the camp for faces—my parents, Pudi. We sank into the stupor of refugee life. The nights were freezing. The days burned our skin. Mosquitoes attacked our eyes. People started streaming in from Uvira, approaching Claire, and saying, "I saw your husband die. He was working in an area where everyone died." Many people seemed to believe, when they arrived, that they were going from danger to safety, that this camp was a stop on the way to somewhere better and eventually back home. The human mind is an amazing, resilient, self-deceptive thing.

Every day, more white-and-blue trucks arrived, with more displaced families. For a week, people continued telling Claire that Rob was dead. Then the story changed: He was alive. They'd seen him last night, just outside the gate.

"No," Claire said. "My husband died in the war. Everybody said he died in the war. How can you say you've seen him?"

But then another truckload would arrive, more people asking for Claire. The message became specific. *Be at the gate at 10:00 p.m.* Rob would pay off the guard. A man in a taxi with dark windows would shout out our names. We would jump the fence and he would drive us away.

That night we waited. A man called Claire's name. She swaddled Mariette in several wrappers and threw her over the six-foot-high fence, chicken wire topped with barbed wire, then climbed over herself. But I was slow, and by the time I was ready to climb over, the guard had changed. The man in the taxi shouted to me that he'd return the next night.

Claire drove off. I curled up on our patch of dirt, terrified. My fear of abandonment had been realized. Yet later that night a guard came and found me, and told me that Claire was waiting with the man in the taxi. I cut my thigh on a piece of barbed wire when climbing over the fence.

WE TOOK A TAXI TO KIGOMA, where we joined more of Rob's extended family in an overcrowded compound. They'd lived there for decades. Everybody slept on the floor. The men ate in one group, the women in another. There was not enough food, so we drank lots of tea.

One afternoon Rob's mother, who'd left Zaire after us, with Rob, prepared a pot of tea and gave it to Claire to serve to the men and boys sitting around the table. Tea, too, was in short supply. Mama Nepele placed only spent tea leaves inside the pot.

Rob had barely looked at me since we'd arrived in Kigoma. He had not fled Zaire as a refugee. He still had papers from CARE that allowed him to enter Tanzania. But he had no home. He'd abandoned his whole life. He was unwanted, one of us.

Claire delivered the pot of tea to the table and returned to the kitchen. A few minutes later Rob yelled, "Claire, come here!"

She entered, silent.

"What kind of woman are you who doesn't even know how to make tea?" Rob shouted. "How come you can't make tea? You think we're going to drink water?" Claire froze. "What kind of woman are you?" Rob was performing for the benefit of men in the room. "This is an embarrassment. Disgusting."

Mama Nepele walked out of the kitchen and placed her body between her son and Claire.

"Rob, what about the tea?" she said with a simmering fury. "I am the one who made the tea. Why do you have to humiliate your wife in front of everyone?" He did not answer. "How do you expect young boys to respect your wife?"

Claire left the dining room. Rob said nothing. Later that week immigration police started knocking on houses in Kigoma, rounding up refugees and taking them back to camp. Claire convinced Rob that we needed to move on.

WE ARRIVED AT THE BUS station late at night because we didn't want to be seen by the immigration police. We carried no bags, just wore layers and layers of clothing. I had on three pairs of underwear, tights with pants over them, and a long skirt on top of all that, plus three shirts, a blue sweater, and a really ugly short scarf, like a shrug. We tried to look presentable. We couldn't look like we were fleeing.

Claire sewed almost all of her money into the waistband of her pants. She left out just enough to bribe people as needed.

We had no real plan, but Claire had heard there was a better camp in Malawi, a camp that was not in the middle of nowhere, that had tents and enough latrines. A camp farther away from the conflict. "Better" meant farther away from the war.

The bus line we rode to Malawi was fancy, or at least fancy to us by then. It catered to the safari crowd. Each Twiga bus had lions or giraffes or some other big African animal painted on the outside. Inside, each window had its own curtain. There were bathrooms and televisions too.

Claire bribed the driver to let us board early. That way we'd be safe until the police entered the bus to check papers at the Malawi border. Once the bus started to move, Claire handed me a brown paper bag filled with sweet bread and milk. But I refused to eat. I thought I was punishing Claire for not warning me that we were leaving, for having all the control.

Every hill we passed, every valley, the landscape grew bleaker—both my internal world and outside. The pink jacaranda gave way to desert palms, which gave way to mesquite. We moved so fast. I did not feel lost, as "lost" implies that there's a place where you will feel found and that, for me, did not exist. I was just a feather, molted and mangled, drifting through space. I tried to maintain the illusion that I kept in my mind a legible map, that I could find my way home. But whenever I tried to think back through the landmarks we'd passed, I just saw people screaming. I heard the sounds of guns and bombs and felt fire.

"In Malawi they have the biggest trees," Claire told me a few hours into our bus ride, "with the biggest, most beautiful mangoes you've ever seen." I knew she was lying. She had never been to Malawi before.

I STILL, MIRACULOUSLY, HAD MY Mickey Mouse backpack, with my marbles and my rocks. Allowing me to keep it seemed to be one of Claire's few concessions to the idea that I should be given any special indulgence for being a child.

One of my rocks was from Lake Tanganyika—it was layered and flaky, like mica. Another was from Tanzania—it was sharp and red. In my pack I also carried a few colored pencils, a notebook, my marbles, and an extra sweater. The sweater was blue and unraveling. I liked to chew on my clothes, especially loose strands of yarn and threads. Claire told me I had to stop or my teeth would rot.

The bus driver played a single video: *The Gods Must Be Crazy*. I didn't speak English but I still watched it, this story of a Kalahari bushman who finds a Coke bottle that's been tossed out of an airplane, and how trying to dispose of it nearly ruins his life. The movie was long and bizarre, and people kept laughing, and my sole response to it was: He leaves his family and his whole world for *this*? The other passengers clapped when the movie finished. Outside it was pouring rain. The driver played the movie again.

Rob, as well as Claire, didn't have valid papers to enter Malawi, so the two of them got off the bus near the river that formed the border with Zaire, to avoid the police. They hoped to find a way to row themselves across. Mariette and I stayed in our seats onboard—Claire figured no one would harass two children alone.

Mariette was now seven months old, unblemished and perfect. She never cried. She'd never bled or been scratched. An hour passed, two, then three. Mariette stayed asleep. If anyone tried to talk to me I planned to remain silent, to pretend I did not understand whatever language was being spoken.

Claire was right: the soldier who boarded the bus asked everybody for papers and ignored me and Mariette. A short while later, Claire and Rob returned. They looked awful. Claire winced when she sat. She could hardly move.

She didn't tell me they'd been beaten but she had a look. She did not look scared—you could not bring Claire low with fear. Claire refused to let anybody limit her sense of her own possibilities or determine her self-worth. People might think they could take everything from her, that they had taken everything from her. You are a woman. You are a refugee. You cannot go to school. You cannot have a job. You are nothing under our laws. She remained immovable, unswayed. Her eyes, when she boarded the bus, said: *Mess with me one more time and I'm going to make it rain fire.*

She did not want to tell me what had happened. I finally wore her down. At first, she said, the crossing went well. She and Rob found a boat and rowed it to Malawi. But once they were on the shore, soldiers caught them and whipped them with an iron rod. Claire pleaded with them to stop, asking why they needed to beat a refugee, why they needed to beat a woman.

Still the blows continued. Rob remained silent.

"Refugees belong in camps," the soldiers barked. "Why are you not in the camp?"

The beating went on. Claire wanted to give the soldiers nothing, but offered her truth: She could not go back to the camp. She'd left her baby and younger sister on the bus. To prove her point, she pulled a breast out of her shirt and pushed against her flesh until white drops of milk appeared.

After that, the soldiers beat Claire's thighs. They beat her back.

Finally, Claire ripped open the waistband of her pants and gave the soldiers $100. They let her and Rob go.

THE NEW REFUGEE CAMP, DZALEKA, was a former political prison, built on a barren red plateau for people in Malawi who had opposed the British. Refugees here lived not in tents but in hundreds of tiny red-brick structures, the bricks made from the plateau's red dirt, mixed with water, shaped, and dried in the sun.

We were refugee-camp connoisseurs, sad, nationless pros. Dzaleka, with its brick huts, felt ominous but sturdy. Near the chicken-wire gate was an office building where refugees could register with the Red Cross in the vain hope that some official agency might have news about their families. The rest of the sprawling camp was overcrowded, so we were moved into the office building. We slept with twenty people in a single room.

The luckiest of our roommates slept on or under one of the tables. A table created at least a bit of separate space. We ate rice and peanut butter and traded whole peanuts for laundry soap. I spent all day, every day, with Mariette, sitting in the shade near the gate, watching with ambition, if not hope. I wanted my parents to walk in. A nice woman helped me acclimate to life in Dzaleka: Here's where you do your laundry, here's when and how to shower. The showers were the most dangerous place in camp, the favored hunting ground of the most depraved men.

Rob still had one good outfit, so each day for the first week he got up, put on his nice striped shirt, shined his brown leather shoes, and set off to find the camp director, to see if he could get work. By noon, Rob returned, disappointed and enraged, lay down on one of the tables, and stared at the ceiling. If anyone spoke to him, he yelled. If Claire or I crossed him, he threatened us.

After a week he stopped putting on his good clothes and just dressed in a T-shirt and played cards.

CLAIRE WAS RESTLESS. SHE DID not want to settle in. In a refugee camp, she knew well, others were invested in your suffering. Their jobs and self-worth depended on your continued abasement, on your commitment to residing in a social stratum below them, the same old neocolonial scheme. Many were American and Canadian; some were educated Africans, like Rob. You could see the surprise in aid workers' faces when you upended their worldview by revealing that you, a refugee, spoke five languages or had aced calculus or ran a successful accounting firm.

To be a refugee was to be a victim—it was tautological. And not just a victim due to external forces like politics or war. You were a victim due to some inherent, irrevocable weakness in you. You were a victim because you were less worthy, less good, and less strong than all the non-victims of the world.

Claire's solution to escaping all that was to make money, for bus fare, to get far away from this place. She took entrepreneurial reconnaissance walks every day, scouting for opportunities. One morning she left with my new romper, sold it, and returned with soap, sugar, and rice.

On one of her strolls, she noticed an old Somali woman sitting in front of her crumbling red-brick hut, selling goat meat. Claire saw her opening. The old woman had a good product but she was lazy and tired. She didn't even bother calling out to passersby to try to make a sale.

Claire could, and did, talk to everyone. She spoke Swahili, Kirundi, Kinyarwanda, and French. She started asking people who'd lived in the camp for a long time how she could get a goat. Who did she have to bribe to leave the camp? Who had a basin in which to collect goat blood? Who had a knife?

I spent the days playing peekaboo over people's beat-up luggage. I learned to tie Mariette onto my back by myself. I learned how to wrap the kitenge around the base of Mariette's scalp to support her neck. I learned when it was a good time to ask our neighbor to borrow her tin basin and electric stove so I could give Mariette a warm bath. I learned the right ratio of salt and sugar to mix with the water in Mariette's bottle. I learned how to clean and sanitize the cloth we used for Mariette's diapers.

Claire, meanwhile, studied how the local Malawi women dressed. They wore long skirts and plastic shoes. So Claire found a long skirt and plastic shoes. She tied up her hair like the locals tied their hair.

Given that the camp was split between Christians and Muslims, Claire realized that if she was going to sell goat meat, the butchering process needed to be halal. So Claire approached a man who slept at the mosque inside the camp. "Do you know how to kill a goat?" she asked him.

The man said yes.

Claire said, "Okay, let's go into business. What should I pay you?"

The man asked for the goat head.

Next, Claire told everybody, "Tomorrow I will have a goat!" She sold a few of her remaining blouses and Rob's good outfit. Before dawn the next morning, she dressed in her long skirt and plastic shoes, bribed a guard to allow her to leave for a few hours, and walked out of the camp, through the fields of beans, groundnuts, and soy. She knocked on the door of every house on the dirt road, asking whether they had a goat for sale.

Claire finally saw one in someone's yard. She knocked and said, "How much?"

"Forty," the man said.

She told him that she only had twenty and he took her twenty and gave her a piece of rope to place around the goat's neck. Then she walked back to camp, with her goat, through the fields.

That afternoon the Muslim man butchered the animal. I did not watch.

Then Claire, a huge smile now on her face, set up a kiosk

and called out, "Meat! Meat!" in all the languages she knew. It was the most basic form of commerce possible: food, on a table, in a pile. No ice, no refrigeration. But working as a black-market butcher gave Claire a sense of power. Dzaleka was the same miserable life for everybody, every day. The men played cards, the women cooked and tried to keep things clean.

The next week, Claire bought a goat again. And the week after. She liked walking the dirt roads alone, singing and praying, thinking about something other than hour-to-hour survival. One week the goat she bought ran away from her and she had to chase it all the way back to the house of the farmer from whom she'd purchased it. The farmer's children corralled the goat in the yard and, once again, looped the rope around its neck. Claire walked the goat back to camp.

I WENT TO SEE A Jesus movie about three or four months after we arrived at Dzaleka. By then we'd moved out of the office and into our own dilapidated red-brick hut. The place didn't have a roof, so we covered it with a nylon tent. It had a bed for Claire and Rob, a mat for me and Mariette, and a little privacy.

The movie was playing in the center of the camp, in the open area where we all lined up to collect our rations of corn from the parked trucks. That evening, a Christian charity had arrived with a projector and some chocolate. They tied up a bedsheet, which served as a screen, and all the kids jostled each other to find a place to sit on the dirt with a view.

I was mesmerized—Jesus in his tunic, his long pale nose and smooth hair; all the men with beards. I'd only seen images of skinny Christ nailed to the cross, frozen in his agony. This Jesus walked up in the mountains, preaching to his flock, his loaves and fishes multiplying. I was so happy to see food.

I left before the end because I knew it was getting late, and I arrived home to find Claire and Rob furious. "I looked everywhere for you," Claire screamed.

Behind her, on the bed, I saw nearly all our possessions in neat piles. Beside the door sat a few small bags. Claire hadn't bothered to tell me, but she'd made a plan with some other families who'd slept with us in the office to leave Dzaleka that night. Neither Rob nor Claire would let me look through the piles of stuff on the bed that they'd decided we would leave behind. I hated them.

Before leaving, I grabbed my Mickey Mouse backpack off the bed and stuffed three pairs of underwear into it.

ALL THAT NIGHT WE WALKED. I felt such rage. I'd finally mastered my life here. I knew how to survive—who to borrow soap from when I laundered the clothes, how to sterilize diapers. And now we were walking away.

Claire carried Mariette on her back—I did not—and Claire did not even have Mariette tied on right. Her arms were sticking out. Her legs were sticking out. Mama Nepele warned me never to do that. She said that a baby's exposed arms and legs were how the cold gets in. Claire knew nothing. She never learned even the most basic childcare tasks.

We walked into the farm fields, across the main road,

down miles of dusty footpaths lined with acacia trees, Bruniaceae scrub, and palms. We approached a stream. The rumbling sounded like relief. I cupped my hands to drink. The water was so cold. Claire never spoke while we walked, and she never told me where we were going. She just moved, upright and aggressive, an overstuffed nylon bag in each hand, a sun-bleached cloth wrapped around her head, Mariette tied to her back.

She didn't care if I pouted or if I seethed, or if, in my eight-year-old absurdity, I carried my Mickey Mouse backpack filled with the rocks that I'd collected over the past two years to keep track of where we'd been.

Claire also didn't care if I was thirsty, exhausted, hungry, hot, despairing, confused, or lonely. She didn't care if the grass cut my legs or if, now that I'd outgrown my Converse sneakers, my cheap plastic shoes burned my feet.

Claire didn't care if Rob terrified me. She understood that Rob, too, had lost everything—his job, his home, his self—and now that he was a refugee, like us, he wanted to broadcast his pain. He hit Claire, he drank the last sips of our water. He carried nothing but his own food.

Claire didn't care, or at least didn't show me that she cared, that Rob scared her too.

I could feel Claire's fear, all the adults' fear. It was strung head to toe in their bodies, thin and brittle as pencil lead. They whispered, in jagged voices, about avoiding the Malawi immigration police.

Before dawn I heard Rob say that he thought we'd crossed the border into Mozambique. That made no sense to me. I had always assumed that a border was, if not a fence, at least a long ditch, a crack in the earth. I'd seen the lines on maps: black, unambiguous, imposing. I never considered those were made up.

I scanned the ground for clues, for signs of change, exotic plants, strange animals, glinting rocks. Along with geological specimens I wanted to collect memories, images to store and save so that when I saw my mother, my brother, or my father I could tell them, in detail, what I'd seen.

I fantasized, daily, of walking into a market, seeing my mother, and telling her I'd buy her anything there. My brother would be at the market too. I'd give him the biggest hug, then buy him popcorn and gum.

We walked over shells and bullet casings. Finally we reached the main road. Tall grass grew from splits in the pavement. I never imagined that civilization could look so forlorn.

WE REACHED A BUS STOP, where our group sat down to rest, in the morning cool air, under a tree. Nobody talked or moved. We waited for hours. Time mattered only to our stomachs. The goal was just to survive. We'd made it through the night, now to make it through the day.

We'd eaten all the roasted groundnuts Claire had packed for food. All that remained was Mariette's soft cassava porridge. I was so hungry but willed myself to fall asleep by imagining the self-loathing I'd feel when Mariette screamed in hunger.

The bus arrived shortly after daybreak—a military bus with almost no seats. A few of the men stood. The rest sat on the floor with the women and children. I compressed myself into a ball, bouncing and jolting with each pothole, so angry and desperate to stay inside myself that I refused to unfurl.

Claire nudged me when the sun was almost down. We'd reached Tete, the capital of one of the provinces in Mozambique. We all got off the bus. I sat, in a stupor, beside our luggage with Claire, Mariette, and a couple of other women.

After a few minutes I snapped out of my fog in horror. I'd left my Mickey Mouse backpack on the bus. I could see across the depot that the bus was still there. I knew exactly where the backpack was. I'd hidden it in a slot between one of the few seats on the bus and a side wall so no one would steal it while I slept.

I asked Rob, in the nicest, calmest voice I could muster, if he would please go get it for me. He refused. I begged Claire. She looked at Rob and then shook her head at me, no. I asked the other women. They would not go either. No one would go. No one would risk being caught by the immigration police.

I stood up and took a few defiant steps toward the bus myself. Rob grabbed my wrist. "No. NO," he hissed. I felt the threat of his violence, just as he wanted me to. "No one cares. Leave it."

8

I walked onstage, my school backpack containing just two objects, as per my drama teacher's instructions. The first was a picture of Mariette and Freddy standing in front of the gate at our first apartment in Chicago. They looked so incredibly sad. Mariette stared straight at the camera and her eyes had nothing behind them. Freddy was two—so tiny, perfect, and worried. That photo still makes me cry.

The second object was my pillow, which had a lavender sachet inside the case. Mrs. Thomas had bought me the sachet in hopes of chasing away my nightmares. Each evening she microwaved the little silk pouch and inserted it, warm, next to the down. I loved our ritual but it didn't work. I hardly slept.

The objects were for my eleventh-grade improv class. Our instructor had given us a simple assignment: present yourself to the group using only two possessions. The exercise made me agitated and insecure. I'd been doing theater since the seventh grade and my teachers always told me I was brilliant. They cast me as the star in *Les Mis*. I never doubted them. I didn't want to consider that I was given roles out of pity or consolation. But by high school they started letting me in on the truth: I was a terrible actress. I tried to mimic expressions of anger or joy, but I never accessed my own emotions. My performances were mechanical and flat.

For the two-object assignment, I asked my teacher for more precise instructions. I wanted to know who to pretend to be. "Just express yourself!" she said. "You're not acting—just be yourself. This is going to set you free."

On the appointed day, the stage was set with a twin bed. When it was my turn, I walked onstage and set the pack down as if to do my homework. That's who I was, right? A kid who came home from school and did her homework. But I could feel that I was failing—communicating nothing, revealing nothing of myself—and I hated to fail, so I tried a new tack. I took my pillow out and placed it on the bed, lay my head on it, and stared at the picture of Mariette and Freddy.

Then I just lost it. All the anger inside me erupted. I threw the pillow to the floor, ripped the sheets off the bed, found my cell phone and called Rob, for real. He didn't pick up, so I left a raw, ranting message, telling him my truth, at last: He was supposed to have protected us from so much terror, and he hadn't. He'd failed. He'd abandoned us. He'd caused terror of his own, and we were so hurt.

"I forgive you," I said. "I can do that: I forgive you. But

I will never trust anyone ever again. I will never put my life in anyone's hands, never again."

I sobbed until my teacher called me offstage.

My classmates avoided me after that.

BY THE TIME I WROTE my essay for the Oprah contest, we knew my parents were alive. Claire had kept in touch with World Relief, the agency that brought us to the United States.

One day, while she was at the Chicago office, she met a Rwandan woman from the same village as our uncle, my mother's eldest brother. That uncle was a priest and the only person in our family we believed to be alive. He'd moved to Belgium before the genocide, as had the children of this woman.

Claire ran across the street to a convenience store and bought a phone card. She gave it to the woman to call her children to see what they knew.

It turned out that my uncle had since returned to his home village in Rwanda and was a priest there. So the woman made another call. A few moments later she handed Claire a slip of paper with the phone number of my uncle's church.

The next morning Claire called. The priest was taking a nap.

Claire called back an hour later—still napping.

The third time Claire called, the priest was awake.

I was at the Thomases', in my bedroom with the built-in bookcases, my cheerleading uniform on the floor. Claire told our uncle her name.

He didn't believe her. He said, "Those children died a long time ago."

Claire told him our parents' names.

He said, "No, no, no."

Claire said, "Uncle, it's me. My nickname was Pupusi."

He gasped, then erupted in joy.

Claire was terrified to ask about our parents. So many people were murdered. How could you ask if your family was alive? It was hard to want to know.

Our uncle saved Claire the trouble. "Your parents— they are still alive, still in Kigali," he said, once he composed himself. "They are still alive, but their lives have really changed."

My father had lost his business. Rebels had stolen our house. My parents had no phone. Our uncle gave Claire the number of our aunt, our mother's youngest sister. She lived two hours from Kigali. My uncle said he'd tell our aunt to visit my parents the following morning with her phone.

THE NEXT DAY I SKIPPED school and took the L to Edgewater and sat in Claire's apartment. I hated going there. Rob cheated on Claire. He hit her, he told her she was ugly, he made her feel worthless. I watched in silence as Claire dialed.

"Hi, Mama," I heard her say. I walked out of the room.

My mother fainted, and Claire called back. I could not bear to listen to them.

"Yes, Mama, Clemantine is alive too. We were refugees for a long time. A very long time. All over. We're in America now."

Claire and my mother spoke like strangers. No one knew what to say. My mother told her Pudi was alive.

My sister lied and said she'd married a nice man. She tried, unsuccessfully, to sound joyful when she told my mother she had three kids. There was no masking how wrong that was. Three children by age twenty-two was way off the family plan.

It felt surreal and awful. I'd lost track of who I was and who we were to each other. None of us were the same people who'd lived together in that house in Kigali. Those people had died. We had all died.

For years I'd told myself that I would remember all the places I'd been and all the things I'd seen and I would tell my mother. I'd share everything about my life.

Now I decided not to tell her anything at all.

9

All night long, every night, I imagined how I would fight if it ever happened.

I saw teeth. Teeth as my weapon. My teeth, my nails, my hands, my kick. I saw myself kicking and biting. I had never bitten anyone in my life.

I saw myself propelling my body into motion—physically, verbally, emotionally. I saw the way I had to stand. The way I had to glare. I had to project, *Do not mess with me,* and not just with the control I used for women—with a wild fury. *You cannot take what is mine.*

I had to be impermeable, self-sufficient, and I practiced this in my waking hours too. I didn't trust or accept help, especially from men, because when people extend their help to you, they feel you owe them. They believe they have the right to take advantage of you later. When you are at your lowest, they will say, *Well, remember I gave you those beans?* When you have nothing, nothing at all to give, they will say: *I need you to repay me now.*

MY RAGE AT LOSING MY backpack was dark red. Everything in Mozambique was dark red. The men walked off into the town of Tete to find help. I tried to fall asleep again to escape, for a few moments, the boils of my sadness. The moon rose—the men were still gone. The moon crossed the sky—no one returned.

Claire's face hardened. I could not be awake for this life. Then, from the shadows, a few women in black dresses emerged. They brought us sweet bread and water, and started talking to Claire in a language that sounded nearly like French.

They gathered their dresses—nuns' habits, it turned out—and sat with us on the ground. One noted my scowl and patted my hand. A few hours passed. The men did not return. When the moon was high, a few more nuns arrived with the news that the immigration police had caught three men, including, presumably, Rob. Rob, along with the rest of us, had crossed the border illegally, so he was put in jail.

We walked with the nuns down a side road to a former soldiers' camp, a half dozen sturdy green tents. The nuns offered us more bread and water, plus jam, candles, mosquito repellent, and supplies for Mariette—proper diapers, which I hadn't seen since Zaire, and a bottle of formula.

Inside the tent a dog slept on the cardboard slabs intended to be our beds. I stood outside. It started raining.

When, soaked, I finally entered, the dog left and I lay down on the soggy cardboard and fell asleep.

In the morning the nuns walked us to the prison. The border patrol had jailed the men in one room, the women in another. For a while we sat on a bench in the hallway, where mosquitoes attacked our ears and eyes. Claire held Mariette up to a guard, hoping to compel mercy. His face remained blank. Later in the morning, another guard appeared. Together the two men shooed all of us women and children into a windowless room, and locked the door.

The guards only spoke Portuguese. None of us did. For a while Claire and the other women stuck to the two languages everybody understands: smile or cry. Then Claire started screaming. We all screamed.

"Aren't you ashamed?" Claire yelled in Swahili as she banged on the door. "Do you know how hungry these children are? We walked from my country at war."

I joined her, yelling, "Yeah. Yeah. Yeah," her self-appointed chorus.

I was still so furious about my backpack, but I felt relieved to be away from Rob. I suspected Claire was relieved too. Still, we needed him. Two girls and a baby—Rob was a shield, our barrier against more predatory men.

Eventually the chief of immigration unlocked the door. He had a kind face. He spoke in Swahili, telling Claire that he, too, was a refugee, from Tanzania. Claire told him the simplest version of our story. After that he gave us bus fare south to Maputo, the capital of Mozambique, where, he said, we must stay at the refugee camp.

We slept that night on the cardboard at the nuns' camp. The next day the chief of immigration released the men.

. . .

BY THAT POINT I KNEW that Rob wanted to leave me behind. Unlike Claire, he did care about my emotions—they infuriated him.

I couldn't look at Claire. I didn't want her to see my anger, or how desperate I'd become. In Maputo immigration officers met our bus and took us to a camp, this one run by Italians, and surprisingly nice. The camp was set up like a hostel—a long barracks with lines of cots. Claire and Rob had a mattress and sheets. Mariette and I slept on the floor.

I was happy to be there, to be treated like a person, a normal person with normal human needs. We received dried milk, tomato sauce, bread, and toothpaste. Sometimes we received fish. On Fridays aid workers distributed pasta. I felt safe. The weather was hot, and while I did not risk walking around in my underwear, as the men did, I felt secure enough to wear a tank top.

Still, at night children cried out, "Mama, Mama!" as they drifted into sleep. I hated them for it.

In the morning life felt manageable again.

A few days after we arrived, Claire approached a woman who'd been living in the camp for twenty years. Twenty years, here? That unit of time made no sense. Maputo was only 60 miles from the South African border, 370 miles from Durban. Men who could afford bus tickets would sneak out and cross the border to live in South Africa and work. Yet this woman had lived here, in the camp, more than twice as long as I'd been alive. Claire said to this woman, with her salesgirl charm, "I have this nice bra that can fit you." The woman bought it for ten Mozambican metical, less than twenty cents.

Claire asked another old-timer, a Rwandan man who'd lived at the camp for sixteen years, to accompany her into Maputo. He spoke some Portuguese, and he told Claire that he'd known our aunt who'd died in the conflict, the conflict no one would name. Claire explained nothing to me.

The next day Claire and the man set out for Maputo, an hour away on foot. In town they walked around until Claire found a general store. Claire told her Rwandan chaperone, "Ask the shopkeeper if he wants to do business with me! Tell him I can give him spaghetti from Italy."

The Rwandan man did as told. "This young woman wants to do business with you," he said to the Indian shopkeeper, in Portuguese. "She says she'll bring you pasta from Italy."

The shopkeeper said, "Oh, do you have a sample?"

Claire pulled a box of pasta out of her bag and waited while the shopkeeper inspected it. "How many do you want?" she then asked. "How much will you pay me for half a dozen?"

The shopkeeper offered Claire five metical a box.

That evening, at camp, Claire was on fire. She went around the barracks asking, "Who wants money?" She offered people two metical a box for their pasta. She bought four and the next day returned to Maputo with the Rwandan man. The Indian shopkeeper gave her twenty metical, which, back at camp, she gave to Rob. He took a bus to South Africa the following day.

In the middle of the week Claire returned to Maputo to check on her pasta business. The shopkeeper had sold out.

From then on, each Friday, Claire bought as many boxes of pasta as she could afford from others at the camp, and on Saturday morning she woke up at 4:00 a.m., borrowed a wheelbarrow, and carried her supply into town. With her profits she purchased soap, milk, and candles, which she brought back to camp for me to sell. Now, thanks to Claire, our camp had a small black-market economy.

We had a roof. We had a stove to boil Mariette's water so she would not get sick. That was enough. I wanted to stay. But Claire was determined not to get comfortable. She thought lingering in a good camp was even more dangerous than staying in a bad one. We could not start to believe this life was okay.

10

My survival plan in high school was shoddy, a sheet of plywood nailed over a broken window. This worked well enough for a while: I shut out my family, kept up my routine, worked hard at school.

When I needed a bit more help, I escaped into Toni Morrison. In *Sula,* she described a world full of people I knew: a girl whose laughter carried but whose "adult pain . . . rested somewhere under the eyelids"; a regal black woman who "lost only one battle—the pronunciation of her name"; children "whose loneliness was so profound it intoxicated them and sent them stumbling." She embraced the same deep existential isolation I felt. "Lonely, ain't it?" one of Morrison's characters asks Sula.

"Yes," she says, "but my lonely is *mine.*"

. . .

THEN ONE DAY, WHEN I was in Target with Mrs. Thomas, Claire called to tell me Pudi was very sick. They thought he had meningitis.

I went straight to Western Union to wire all my baby-sitting money to my parents to buy him medicine.

The next day, Friday, after school, I took the train to Claire's apartment, where the two of us spent the weekend waiting for the phone to ring. Claire had recently left Rob. His abuse had become intolerable. She had no furniture. It didn't matter. We sat on a mattress on the floor.

The plan was that my mother would call if it was not fine. We waited and waited. My mother called. Claude—Pudi—had died.

Pudi was then twenty-two years old. I never knew him as a young man. I never talked to him on the phone—I was so scared. Talking to Pudi would have been talking to a ghost. I never told him that I always thought of him. I didn't say, *I missed you.* Or, *You tried to help me understand a world I would never understand.* Or, *I saved all these things to give you.* I had so much to share with Pudi and nothing at all to share. We all lived lives my parents never dreamed of us having.

I lay back on the mattress and cried an ocean of tears. So many people had been lost, so many people killed. Pudi was the first person that we mourned.

. . .

IN AUGUST 2006, THREE MONTHS after we appeared on Oprah, Claire flew back to Rwanda. She'd become a U.S. citizen a week before we appeared on the show. She found my parents living on the outskirts of Kigali, in a shack. My father wasn't working. He had high blood pressure and diabetes. My mother cooked by herself, no house girls.

Claire took a bus into the city and walked to the embassy, where she was greeted like a star. "It's Claire from Oprah!" the clerk said. Everyone in Rwanda had watched the video of us on TV. It was a feel-good story and lord knows Rwanda needed feel-good stories then.

A genocide museum had been built in the lush lowland that ran through the center of Kigali. The museum contained a detailed, graphic teaching exhibit; a mass grave for 250,000 people; and a wall of names, modeled after the Vietnam Memorial, that, to this day, is nowhere near done. Trying to circumscribe and commemorate the pain of the entire country is not really possible.

The final exhibit in the museum is a film in which traumatized Rwandans talk about forgiving. They say the whole country has to forgive, that they themselves have forgiven. Not long ago, Claire and I sat in the grass in a park near my apartment in San Francisco and fought about forgiveness.

Claire believes that she can and needs to forgive. Her faith is her shield. Hallelujah. Be grateful.

"Rob's cousin, who lost her baby," I said to Claire. "She had all the pain, all the worst pain we can imagine God inflicting on a person. And these men came along and stole from her. They took all she had left. They took her humanity, and we are asking her to forgive?"

Claire listened, unmoved. She said, "I have my own peace. I told myself long ago, no one can take my peace."

"But people need to know, people need to say to themselves, 'I cannot do this thing because this thing is unforgivable. I cannot decide my wife is a cockroach. I cannot decide my neighbor is a snake. I cannot kill my wife. I cannot kill my neighbor. I cannot make others less than human and then kill them. This is unforgivable. This will never be forgiven.' There should never be a pass."

Claire stayed quiet. When she spoke she said, "Let's talk about Rwanda"—a first. "There are some people, they had kids and somebody came and killed all their kids and the killer survived. There are children, they lost their parents, everything, and the killers survived. And Rwanda is peaceful right now. Do you think Rwanda could be peaceful right now if no one would forgive?"

I understand that forgiveness is utilitarian, that it is likely even the missing piece in my life, the keystone that will allow me to balance and stabilize and keep the bricks of my life from tumbling down. But I can't do it. To me it feels false.

"The thing is, Rwanda is peaceful but it's in people's hearts. It's in people's hearts and it's going to come out."

"Forgive or forget," Claire whispered.

"Forget? There's no forget. The damage is done. It will come back. Those lines were crossed and we can't go back. Husbands killed their wives, wives killed their husbands. People told us, 'Those other people over there, we do not want them. They are cockroaches,' and we believed them. In their minds, that was okay. We have to say, 'I am responsible. We are responsible. They are responsible. This happened.' Right now, when we are sleeping, we see it in our dreams.

We make a painting and we think it's beautiful and the monster is right there."

Claire said, "Can we talk about something else?"

THE CONSULATE GAVE CLAIRE VISAS for my mother and my youngest sister. Claire was back on her home turf, once again an effective dealmaker. But she didn't have money to buy them plane tickets to Chicago—not yet.

So she flew back to the United States and returned to work. She still worked nine- or ten-hour days, six days a week. When she was not cleaning hotel rooms, she cleaned houses. It had been so hard for Claire to find a self here. Rob spent his paychecks on his girlfriends when they were together. He beat Claire; he tore her down. Claire later told me the degradation of that marriage was worse than the degradation of refugee life.

In December, Claire returned to Rwanda, to try again to bring my mother back to Chicago to live with her. Claire called me from Kigali. She didn't have the money to buy my mother a plane ticket; she'd known she didn't when she left. She'd flown there trusting God would help her find it.

The conversation was tense. Claire knew I didn't have that kind of money. I told her I would not ask the Thomases. Then she reminded me about my boyfriend, Troy, and his father.

Troy and I didn't have much of a physical relationship. He was kind and generous, and we kept each other company. His parents had split up. He felt really lonely in his house. Often he came with me to Claire's and helped with the kids. He cooked while I cleaned. He did the laundry. He invited Freddy to his football and basketball games. Troy and I balanced each other. He saw all the lies and hypocrisy in the world; I wanted to stay numb. One day his father gave him a car and he refused the gift. I later read *Into the Wild* to try to understand him, why he deprived himself of things. Claire's point was: Troy's father had once told me that if my parents ever had the opportunity to move to the United States, he'd help pay for the tickets.

I hated asking. The whole dynamic of giving and receiving made me tense. I was nineteen, a kid but not a kid, and already the recipient of profound generosity. I didn't want to become a charity. Claire, too, had never wanted to be saved. Other refugees we knew made the opposite play—they wore ratty pants and no shoes, to broadcast their need. But Claire didn't want the low rung in a hierarchy.

Claire had an intuitive sense of the postcolonial aftershocks, the lingering effects of outsiders coming in to save, enlighten, and modernize Africa. The colonists, the aid workers, the NGOs—they're all in a single progression: paternalistic foreigners, assuming they are better and brighter, offering shiny, destabilizing, dependence-producing gifts. How can one accept anything from so-called rescuers when their predecessors helped your people destroy one another?

It's not enough for outsiders to want to atone for their sins. They need to look at themselves, their history and biases, and make a plan for how not to repeat their crimes. Our minds are malleable. Our minds can be possessed— possessed so gradually that we don't even realize we've lost control. The German leaders had practiced the tactics they used on the Jews in the Holocaust in Namibia almost four decades earlier. The violence and degradation were systematic. Those Europeans considered their race to be superior to the Herero and Nama ethnic groups, and they became facile at mass-killing techniques: sealed-off water holes in the desert, death camps, whips.

But Claire, determined to fly back to America with our mother, worked her jujitsu on me and made a convincing argument that my mother was too fragile, and would be too overwhelmed if Claire returned to Chicago solo to earn more money and our mother had to emigrate to the United States by herself.

Claire's own return flight to Chicago was leaving in two days. So I made the call. I was mortified, but a few minutes later Troy's father was talking with Claire in Kigali.

They conferenced-in the airline. Claire gave the ticketing agent my mother and my sister's information; my boyfriend's father gave the ticketing agent his credit card number.

By that point it was very late in Rwanda. The next morning Claire told my mother she had airline tickets for her.

My mother asked, "Where did you get the money?"

Claire said, "God."

I WAS STILL TOO TERRIFIED to deal with my mother, so I avoided Claire's apartment.

My mother tried to help Claire with her house and her children, but there were endless misfires. My mother didn't reset the time on her watch, so two days after arriving she woke Claire's kids up in the middle of the night to get them ready for school.

My mother didn't know English and Claire's children understood very little Kinyarwanda, so she clapped at them to go take showers or to clean up their rooms, and this drove them crazy. Claire felt infantilized too—my mother wanted Claire to fall under her care again: to cook for her, to run the home.

Neither Claire nor I had been a child in such a long time. Claire did not want to be mothered. She wanted to make money. The two of them crushed each other. Claire would cook and my mother would say, "I don't like my chicken fried." Or Claire would open her closet and give my mother clothes and my mother would say, "I don't wear this kind of blouse. I don't like these shoes." Those small moments undid Claire. This was not the reunion she had expected. Often she walked out of her house and sat by Lake Michigan, trying to breathe.

A FEW MONTHS LATER CLAIRE returned to Rwanda once again, for my father and other two siblings. The church had raised the money for the plane tickets.

This time she brought my father with her to the American embassy in Kigali. He was so destroyed, but he kept in his wallet a photo from the day of the Oprah taping, and when the consulate asked my father if he had family in the United States, he reached in and pulled out the picture of himself, Claire, me, and Oprah. The consul nearly fainted. "Oh my goodness! Oprah! Can I make a copy?"

The consul gave my father a ten-year visa.

My parents arrived as immigrants, not refugees, which means they had a country. Living in America sounded prestigious. Of course they came. But they were not really capable of planting themselves, digging in, growing roots and branches into the past and future to create a full life. Like Claire, my parents didn't talk about before, or what had happened between before and now. They existed in a never-ending present, not asking too many questions, not allowing themselves to feel, moving forward within the confines of a small, tidy life. They stopped talking whenever Claire or I walked into the room. Perhaps this was inevitable—that we would become permanent aliens, irreparably estranged.

My father was now in and out of the hospital for his diabetes. Claire had eight people living in her apartment—our immediate family plus several cousins—and she was the only one with a job. This was fine, everything was fine. At the beginning of the week she bought a big box of chicken and a bag of rice at World Market. The church dropped off a few grocery bags of staples to supplement that, and everybody tried to make it last.

On weekends, at Claire's house, I'd see my youngest sister, who was six, jump into my mother's lap, as though anybody could just jump into her mother's lap. She'd beg for my mother's attention, like all lucky little girls do.

One night, I sat down at Claire's kitchen table to study for the SATs. My mother, who'd been taking ESL classes, sat down to do her own homework, next to me. It was the first time we'd been still and close together in fourteen years.

The one time I tried to ask my mother what had happened to her during the war had not gone well. She had been cleaning my sister's apartment, which I thought would provide a good distraction. She could keep her eyes on the cupboards she was wiping down, and tell me about her life without the unbearable intimacy of me seeing her face. But as soon as I said, "What happened . . . ," I felt ashamed. The cabinet door started shaking, my mother's hands frantic and trapped, a bird flown through a window who can't escape. Now I see I should have known better. Claire told Mariette almost nothing. What mother could? The contours of pain are not fixed. Suffering expands and metastasizes. Our pain stays in our own hearts and fills our loved ones' as well.

My mother hardly slept anymore. She just focused on her children and grandchildren, and the dozens of other neighborhood kids. She kept lists. She remembered everybody's birthday and gave each child as many dollars as their age. Her punishments grew soft.

As I practiced for the SATs, my mother bowed her head and studied her ESL workbook, pausing and deliberating over each word, as if taking a final exam. Her dark skin didn't match mine. Her hair was short and tight against her head—I remembered it as long. Her fingernails were chipped. Her lips were parched. The fantasy of reunion was a lie. No lights, no camera angles, no makeup could restore the time we'd lost and the relationship we could have had. The only things about my mother that conformed to my memory and felt congruent with the mother I knew were her cheekbones and the white rosary she wore around her neck.

I ran to the bathroom and turned on the shower full blast. After twenty minutes, Claire knocked on the door.

"You are not taking a bath. Why are your eyes red?" she asked harshly. "Have you been crying? What happened?"

11

I could see fear in Claire's face. Fifteen of us were packed into the coyote's car. He drove crazy fast, in the dark with no headlights, and I was sure we were going to hit a tree. Claire had heard that in South Africa you could make money everywhere. You could get a job. So we were fleeing Mozambique. I, age eight, crouched in the car's footwell. To contain my fright I focused on my hands. In the lines of my palms I saw a picture of an old woman.

The coyote stopped the car at a hut in a cluster of trees and gave us dried meat, bread, and water. Then we started walking across a nature preserve. The sky was orange, that orange I hated. I saw snakes—the coyote hadn't told us there would be snakes.

We walked for miles. Claire carried Mariette in front.

I missed the weight of Mariette's body. When we finally arrived at an electric fence, a section near the bottom had been cut out and we crawled under.

A truck waited for us a few miles away. I sat in a seat now, holding Mariette. We drove and drove, toward the lights, the little yellow lights from the streetlamps and the houses.

I had not seen faraway twinkling lights in so long. Everywhere we'd lived had been dark and torn by war. The lights made me think about bread and jam, bread and butter, french fries. I asked Claire when we were going back home. She gave me a hard look and didn't answer.

I knew she didn't like me. I was a burden. I was terrified she'd leave me behind.

SOUTH AFRICA LOOKED SO BEAUTIFUL. We spent the night in an abandoned office building taken over by those who'd fled the conflict in Zaire.

Down a long hallway we met a woman who cooked us *ugali* and lent us a blanket. She made chicken but gave us only a few bites of the wings. The rest of the meat and the gizzards were reserved for the men.

The next day, Claire set out to find Rob. South Africa was jubilant and tense, filled with pride. Mandela was president. Claire found Rob living in a township in Mayville, sharing one room with four families. He had a job cutting hair. It was a life.

As refugees, we could go to the Department of Home Affairs and get six-month visas. You could do this multiple times. We didn't have to fear arrest. But Claire wanted to move on. She thought we'd have more opportunities in the coastal city of Durban, which was gleaming and lined with beaches and piers.

Claire always taught me: *Everything is yours, everything is not yours. The world owes you nothing; nobody deserves more or less than the next person.*

Even as a refugee she always kept one dignified outfit—early on, a crisp white blouse, well-fitting flared jeans, short black boots; later, a brown suit—so she could present herself to anybody, anywhere, as a smart, enterprising young woman, period. She asked for no pity, no permission. She was a fact of life, an equal. Nobody needed to know more.

She had a routine by now. You go. You find someone who speaks the language. You put on your best outfit and you knock on doors asking for opportunity, never for money. You get a job. You work hard. You don't steal.

In Durban, Claire found a Tanzanian who knew Zulu and she persuaded him to act as her interpreter. She put on her white blouse. She entered a wealthy neighborhood. She knocked on a door. When a man answered, Claire instructed her Tanzanian interpreter, "Tell him that I would like a job."

The man who answered the door said to come back in the morning.

So Claire did. She arrived the next morning, again in her white blouse and good jeans; the man's wife gave her a basket of clothes to wash, by hand. Claire was now the house girl, like the girls my mother had employed in Kigali.

The family could easily have afforded a washing machine, but that wasn't the custom here, so Claire hand-washed clothes for five hours—five children lived in the house—regretting that she had never allowed my mother to teach her these mundane skills. Claire, after all, was not going to need them. She was going to McGill. Now, this. But the woman returned from work and paid Claire well, and told her to come back in three days.

Meanwhile, I hung out with Mariette. We lived in a room in an apartment building, not a camp, but I was an outcast. One day the kids in the neighborhood took pee and froze it and told me it was a popsicle and said that I needed to eat it.

I threw it down and ran away.

CLAIRE PRETENDED TO READ ZULU newspapers on a bus so nobody would think she was a foreigner and harass her. We attended a Baptist church. Claire didn't really understand English, but she cried a lot in church. She loved the singing and the hymns. One Sunday, as we walked out of church, we saw a white Afrikaans woman looking at us. She was big, beautiful, strong, and heavy, and she wore a long dress like a priest's robe.

She came up to Claire and said, "Refugee?"

Claire said, "Refugee."

The woman said, "Yes."

Claire said, "Yes." Claire's English was limited to *yes, no, good morning,* and *good afternoon.* She often just repeated whatever the other person said. I don't know why this woman singled Claire out, but as soon as Claire said yes she motioned for us to follow her.

Her house was about three blocks away, lined with

floral wallpaper, filled with floral couches and curtains. She walked in, opened her refrigerator, and started pulling out fish, beef, chicken, and pork. She set the food on the table, along with plates and fancy napkins, and then she scooped vanilla ice cream into a bowl and watched me eat it. She saw the child in me that no one else seemed to see.

The next week Claire, Rob, Mariette, and I returned to church and followed the Afrikaans woman, Linda, home again. This time her house smelled like curry. She sat down with all of us to eat. Linda was big and Claire was small, and Linda gave Claire an armful of clothes that were all far too large, but it didn't matter. It was such a relief to be cared for.

The third time we visited, Linda motioned to her breast. She'd had cancer and a mastectomy. She showed us her scar. It looked like a map.

After that, the church collected a monthly allotment of food for us. Linda helped us find our own tiny apartment and gave us pots and pans. The day we moved in, she came over with a giant bologna and we made bologna sandwiches with tomato and mayonnaise.

The apartment was on the third floor, across the street from a brothel, and I learned about sex by watching the women who worked there. An older girl who lived in the building explained to me what was going on. One day, in our apartment, she said to me, "You've never been kissed. I'll kiss you."

I said, "I'm never going to kiss anyone."

NO WALKING, NO CAMPS, NO MURDER. Life felt easy for a time. Rob had stopped cutting hair and now worked making textiles in a factory outside of town, meaning, much to my relief, that he was gone nearly a week at a stretch. Claire got a security job watching guests' cars at a fancy hotel. The older girls in our building taught me the Zulu words for *get away, don't look at me, step off.*

One day Claire came home and said, "Put down the mattress! Put down the mattress!" I put down on the floor the mattress we propped against the wall during the day. Claire started pulling money out of her pockets and throwing it on the bed. "We are rich! We are so rich!" she said. "Pick whatever you want! I will buy you whatever you want."

For months, while Claire kept that job watching cars, I told everybody how rich we were. She bought me a new shirt and shoes. She bought us a whole roast chicken. She bought a bag of chicken gizzards. In Africa, the gizzards are reserved for men. If a wife cooks a chicken and she serves it without saving the gizzard for her man, her husband might leave her. But Claire wanted to taste gizzards.

She brought them home and I fried them. They looked like testicles. But to Claire they tasted like victory. She was eating power.

MARIETTE WAS MY WORLD, MY every day, my beautiful, animated doll. I fussed over her outfits, so people would see how cute she was and want to pick her up. I hovered and overprotected. One day I left a hot plate on the floor, and Mariette thought it was a tiny chair and burned herself through her diaper. I felt such shame.

I wanted a mother, preferably Linda. One day she took

me to register at a school. She promised she'd find someone to look after Mariette so I'd be free during the day. While filling out papers, Linda was informed by the principal that I needed to get a tuberculosis test. I'd been coughing a lot. Linda brought me to the hospital. I was infected and needed to be quarantined.

The hospital scared me but made me feel important and pampered. I had my own bed. Linda brought me flowers. One day a nurse woke me up and wheeled me to a room with giant windows through which I could see the whole ocean. The hospital fed us custard. They fed us rice pudding. At lunch the nurse asked, "Do you want Jell-O? Do you want green beans?"

Linda came in one day with a little backpack and a pencil case with my name embroidered on it. She said, "You can start school here. You can learn to write in here."

AFTER I GOT OUT OF the hospital, we moved again, to be closer to the textile factory where Rob worked, this time up in the townships, a few miles out of Durban, among rows and rows of small houses that all looked alike. Mandela had been elected just three years before and he gave the country such exuberant pride. Music blasted through the township at all hours: hip-hop, Biggie, Papa Wemba, Tupac, Brenda Fassie. I worked so hard to learn all the Zulu words to the Brenda Fassie songs. *Open the gates, Miss Gossip. My baby boy is getting married today.*

The plan for me to attend school fell away. In this neighborhood I needed to look after Mariette. In the morning, I'd tie Mariette to my back and watch all the other children go off to school. In the evening, I watched the men come home from work. The bus picked up and dropped off passengers a little way down the hill. There was one man who was tall and stocky, just like my father, and he wore the same cap. I watched him every day.

Zulu was such a hard language. It included clicks and other sounds I'd never made before, and it required using parts of my mouth that I'd never used. I barely spoke a word aloud for months. Then one day I approached a girl I knew to be the daughter of the tall, stocky man I watched every day as he came home from work. I was so eager to have a friend here, to be integrated into the normal world. I dropped my survivor-girl act just long enough to say to her, in my tentative Zulu, "Your father looks just like my father." She threw a fit. I didn't understand why.

Only later did I realize I'd said, "Your father is my father." I tried to explain to the girl but it was too late.

Claire lost her job watching cars, but she started buying clothes wholesale, purchasing soccer jerseys for twenty-five rand and reselling them in barber shops for fifty. She did the same with jeans.

She still worked as a house girl too. Some days I went with her. We did the laundry first, then we swept, then we ironed, Mariette tied to one of our backs. We never worked outside. Black South Africans didn't want jobs as house girls and boys anymore, and they didn't want black immigrants performing those jobs either. We would have been heckled on the bus and in the township if we'd been seen.

Every day, we cleaned the living room just as Oprah came on TV. Oprah was a goddess to me. She had so many different couches. She wore different clothes every time she appeared. I didn't understand what she said, but I loved the way she walked out into the audience, and I loved the way she held herself when she sat—with enthusiasm, concern, joy, anger, solidarity, skepticism, whatever she needed to evoke. I didn't know that anyone could sit that well.

Claire studied Oprah but did not revere her. She swore that she would meet her someday. "Oprah eats, Oprah sleeps," Claire said. "Me too."

I didn't understand Claire's confidence. My sense of self-worth was so relational. My job, while we watched Oprah, was to polish the cocktail table, and I wanted to get an A. I wanted the owner of the house to walk in, notice the table's gleam, and say, *"Zikomo! Zikomo!"* Thank you so much!

I felt so adrift in the world, so much of the time, so outside any category I knew or wanted to grab hold of to define myself. Claire, Rob, Mariette, and I were nobody's vision of a family. Not even mine.

THEN CLAIRE GOT PREGNANT AGAIN and Rob's reaction to this news was to persuade her to go back to Rwanda with me, but not him, to find our parents.

I detested the idea. We were safe here. We could keep renewing our visas. We didn't have papers to travel abroad. Why would we start moving again, by choice, not just to Rwanda but through one wrecked country after another? Plus, our parents were dead. We hadn't heard anything from them for so long. In my head, they were gone.

"Don't worry, Claire. Rwanda is fine," Rob tried to convince us. "They're not going to hurt a pregnant woman."

Claire didn't want to go either. We had a stable life here,

at times even rich! But Claire, however resourceful, was only seventeen. She never let outsiders reduce her to nothing, yet she thought she had to do what her husband wanted her to do. That was how we were raised. Rob was a tyrant, Claire did know that. But she thought she had to obey him all the same.

I wanted to stay with Linda, preferably as her adopted child, but Claire needed me to take care of Mariette.

I was ten. I knew too much, and that knowledge was heavy, a blanket soaked in muddy water. Before, I didn't know what killing entailed—I didn't even know what it meant. Now I'd seen it, I'd felt it. And it was so much worse than the *Rambo* graffiti of violence that Pudi had painted in my brain all those years ago.

Claire, Mariette, and I rode a bus back north to the forest, back toward hell, and climbed through the electric border fence.

12

One Sunday, while I was in Chicago, in Claire's apartment, I occupied myself with Mariette's hair.

My mother was cooking—garlic, onions, meat, and rice—and trying to hum along to a song on the radio that she didn't know. The windows fogged up from the steam trapped below the low ceiling.

"Ouch! Aunt, you're hurting me!" Mariette said, but all I could think was: *You don't know what pain is.*

"I'm sorry," I said, and I promised not to hurt her again. My mind drifted off to college, scholarships, money— trying to get to a place in life that felt comfortable. My mother continued humming. Her voice sounded unfamiliar.

I felt cold, despite the steam and heat of the stove, so I asked Michele, Claire's youngest, "Milu, could you please get me your soft Miley Cyrus blanket?"

Michele looked at me with disdain. She was comfortable, just then, watching *Eloise*. I found her attachment to comfort garish.

When she finally got up, she said, "I want to be like Eloise, trick people and speak to my mom in French."

I laughed—how cute. Then Mariette, five years older than Michele, crushed her dream. "I am very sorry to tell you," Mariette said to her little sister, "but you're stuck here with us and it will never happen."

Michele began to cry. I patted her head and whispered in her ear, "Don't listen to Mariette. You can live like Eloise if you want."

SOME OF THE HARDEST LINES to navigate were between the African and African American communities. Of course I was African, dark-skinned, and I lived in America—specifically in Illinois, in the heartland. Yet I didn't have any personal history with white Americans. No one had enslaved me or my family. No white banker had kept me or my family from buying a house. My community in a white suburb was exceedingly generous to me.

Meanwhile, Mariette, Freddy, and Michele lived in a different universe. They were growing up in Edgewater, in public housing. They picked up the slang and style of their black friends at school and they blended it with the Swahili or Kinyarwanda they learned at home. Even Claire had an intimacy and a fluidity with African American culture that I lacked. Sometimes she would wear a Missy Elliott sweatshirt; other times a gorgeous wild kitenge, complete with head wrap. She understood well the lives of her neighbors whose families had lived for generations in a system that dehumanized and stole from them. I lived Monday to Friday in a house with a well-groomed lawn and a detached garage. I wore polo shirts and J.Crew. My classmates asked me about my weekends in the exotic "inner city." They always called it that—the inner city. Nobody I knew lived in the inner city. They lived on the city's edge.

Toni Morrison wrote about blacks in America with the same question that defined my whole life: *How do I survive?* Every person I met, every paragraph I read, that's what I wanted to know: *How are you surviving?* She described the strength I was looking for; she called it the strength in the blood. *Playing in the Dark: Whiteness and the Literary Imagination* is not my favorite of her books—*The Bluest Eye* is. But it helped me understand how white American stories depend on certain assumptions about black characters. Most of the black people we studied in school were dead. They had fought a war that was not my war. One day I brought home from school *The Autobiography of Malcolm X*. Mrs. Thomas was in the kitchen, cooking black beans. She looked up with a smile and said, "Blackness is beautiful." The pieces of my identity rattled in my head like loose change.

I KNEW I WAS NOW PRIVILEGED. I had started to forget what it was like to suffer, to worry about basic needs. I had time to think, time to create. I worked hard on bleaching and distressing my jeans, to make them look like Britney Spears's. I bought vintage jackets and sewed pieces of various garments together. I signed up for a John Robert Powers modeling class.

Mrs. Thomas was unhappy that I had enrolled in the course. The classes were out by the airport. I took three trains to get there. For the bargain price of two free classes and then a ridiculous fee, John Robert Powers taught susceptible immigrant girls like me how to put on makeup, how to smile with your eyes, how to walk to sell a pair of pants, how to walk to sell a dress, what to have on your résumé when you sit down for an interview, the importance of wearing nude underwear to photo shoots.

This was during the Abercrombie & Fitch era. All the girls at school wore Abercrombie & Fitch. I did too, and I wanted to see somebody who looked like me in their catalogs. I didn't see me anywhere.

At John Robert Powers, the instructors told all of us immigrants what our modeling options might be based on height, weight, shape, skin tone, what your hands look like, your neck. They told us we had to measure ourselves every month because if your résumé said you were a size four and you showed up at a shoot as a size six, people would be upset. The idea of measuring myself bothered me but I so badly wanted to be recognized. I wanted to be looked at and get paid. I wanted to walk into a room and command the space.

In my class was a tall, muscular Russian volleyball player with blond hair extensions—she wanted to do athletic modeling—and a super-thin Ukrainian with a pixie haircut. The Ukrainian had the best prospects. The rest of us were told: *You can do commercials, you can do Walmart, you can sell perfume in a department store.*

I stuck with the class until the day I dressed up and took the bus to a warehouse for a photo shoot. For twenty minutes I felt glamorous, like the women in the lookbooks Mrs. Thomas received from Neiman Marcus. Then I was told that 5" x 8" prints would cost $100 each, and I felt used and left and never paid.

THE UNITED STATES HOLOCAUST MEMORIAL Museum's Midwest office invited me to a luncheon they were hosting for Oprah. I read my entire Oprah essay for a group of three thousand people.

Lots of strangers started calling, wanting me to talk at their events, to fund-raise, to be their story line.

It felt strange and rewarding to become such a useful character. I could connect the dots between the Holocaust and all the other genocides around the world. When I spoke, I could make people feel like they cared and listened, and yet even the kindest individuals with the best intentions rarely made room in their minds for the particular person I was.

Everyone was always exceedingly genteel to me, but under the careful niceties, I knew I had been given a chore. *Please assume this identity: Oprah's special genocide survivor, long-lost daughter made good.* In that narrative, that brilliant fairy tale, I was the clever child who induced the fairy godmother to bring her parents back to life. I was to fill that slot on the show and in viewers' minds. I was complicit. The title "the Oprah Girl" came with a dramatic story line, a happy ending, and a glamorous costume. At first I went along.

I worked closely with Harpo, Oprah's production company. After the first Holocaust Memorial Museum luncheon, I spoke at the museum in Washington, DC, introducing Elie Wiesel. At the end of that event he said to me, "We shall keep meeting each other." Other speaking invitations followed. And my talks were magic. At the end of each one people were in tears. But they understood nothing—least of all, that I wasn't special. There were so many of me, thousands, millions. I just happened to be the one standing in the room. *Don't cry for me,* I wanted to say. *Cry for them. It will take you a hundred lifetimes to cry for all of them.*

Yet still I posed for photos. I let people take my hands in theirs. They thanked me for sharing my story, my sad, harrowing, inspiring story. I smiled. I always smiled. But underneath I also said to myself, *You have no idea. I shared one second of my life with you. I'm not the poor little kid you think I am.*

THE COLLEGE FINANCIAL APPLICATIONS ASKED: How much do your parents make—and I was like, *Which parents?* Do you have family members who fought in the Civil War— *Which civil war?*

My New Trier High School advisor laughed when I showed him my list of schools: Princeton, Yale, Georgetown. He thought I should aim less high. Everybody did. I was a lousy test-taker. My grades were erratic. My mother cleaned bathrooms at O'Hare airport. The counselor thought I should apply to Lake Forest College and William & Mary.

So I did. I applied to those schools, plus all the schools on my own list. Because of FAFSA, the Federal Student Aid department's free application, the only money I spent was on postage stamps.

I was so anxious to leave my Chicago world—to avoid my parents, Claire. Claire was the person who knew everything, and still, when I heard her talk about her life, I felt I did not exist. I felt underappreciated, nearly erased, in her narrative of how her children were raised. I thought if I ran away from my family I could hide from some of the pain, get to a place where I felt I belonged. Nowhere in my life felt right, so I kept trading up.

That fall I marched in the Macy's Thanksgiving Day Parade. I had been the captain of my team at dance camp and as a result I was invited to march. Mrs. Thomas ordered me the whole mustard-colored outfit—the skirt, the sweater, the shoes, the white gloves. I was supposed to wear nude tights. We couldn't find the right nude. I bought too light a color and dyed them myself.

BY SPRING, THE NEWS ARRIVED: I'd been wait-listed at Yale. I knew by then that there were many more rungs of the ladder and that I could climb them if I was patient, if I observed the right people, watched their gestures, mimicked their conversation.

I also knew the power of my story. So when the admissions office said that there was a chance I could move off the wait-list if they learned more about my situation, I flew out to New Haven. I spent the day in a series of interviews, first talking about Habitat for Humanity, then discussing the book *Infidel,* written by a Somalian woman named Ayaan Hirsi Ali who served in the Dutch Parliament. I'd just read the book. Ali's personal story was both so brutal and so typical for a Somalian girl. Her genitals were cut. She was forced to marry. As an adult she rejected her Muslim faith and wrote this blistering feminist critique of Islamic culture. Then finally I just came out with it and told the dean of admissions that I thought I belonged there, at Yale, among the world's future leaders.

It was all so arbitrary: *You should be killed, you should stand in line for food for seven hours, you should be fabulously educated and heaped with praise.*

I told the dean that if people at Yale wanted to make the world a better place, I could tell them what to fix.

A week later the dean called. "I have good news and not so good," he said. "The good news is you've been accepted at Yale. But, the bad news . . ." I inhaled. "Looking at your writing especially, I think you can use some more classes to help you to manage the writing and workload."

"Yes, I'll take classes," I said, jumping in. "In fact I took classes for writing this past summer."

The dean slowed me down. "You might have to do a little bit more," he said. "The type of thing we're talking about is maybe taking writing classes at Northwestern for a few semesters. Or, I was just talking to someone from a boarding school called Hotchkiss and I took the liberty of sending them your application. They'd be very keen on having you there."

I felt spun around and deflated, a balloon spasmodically losing gas. I needed to stay in high school? I was twenty. I was over it. My first, emotional response was preposterously spoiled: *No way, I don't want to do that.* But I pulled myself together. This was the most privileged hardship possible.

13

I saw a father on the bus to the Mozambique border drinking Fanta with his daughter. I wanted so badly to be that girl, to be casually drinking soda on a trip with a parent, though I no longer imagined a real reunion possible if we returned to Kigali. Everything about my body was different. I was nine. I'd lost most of my baby teeth and grown in new ones. I had muscles. I had scars.

I refused to sit with Claire. She was just as happy not to sit with me anyway. She hated my whining and self-pity. So while I jostled Mariette on my lap in the back of the bus, Claire, five months pregnant, sat up near the driver on a jump seat that folded down into the center aisle. Every square inch of the bus was packed with people and bags, the space dense and alien to its surroundings, a submarine in the terrestrial ocean of dust, farmland, oleander, milkweed, agave, lantana, and date palms. The only thing that gave me solace about our journey back north through East Africa was the fact that we'd be passing through Zaire. Zaire was the one place, other than South Africa, that had felt inviting, the one other country where we'd had what felt like a family, where a half dozen women brought me dresses already ironed for church.

But when we arrived, nothing was the same. The war had destroyed Kazimia. The city looked toppled and covered in ash, like a child had kicked over and burned a building-block town. The lake was still deep blue, the ancient palm trees still stately. A few guileless flowers bloomed. Rob's family huddled in his uncle's house, starving. Instead of welcoming us with stew and fish, they served us sweet potato leaves, cut into strips and boiled, with no oil and no salt. I felt so exhausted and so depressed. We left South Africa for this? When we were last in Zaire, people served sweet potato leaves only to pigs.

We had been gone three years.

LIFE HAD BEEN RUBBED AWAY. The electricity was cut off. Many water pumps were dry. You couldn't fish from the shore, you couldn't fish on the lake in a boat, you couldn't hang out on the rocks after you washed—the soldiers wouldn't let you. A curfew barred anybody from leaving the house after 5:00 p.m. and before 7:00 a.m., so you couldn't be out during the time when you'd catch fish anyway.

The lazy afternoons swimming, the dashing clothes on Friday nights, the goofy dancing to the TV in the yard—

that Zaire was gone. The country was now called Democratic Republic of Congo. There were so many soldiers from so many countries. We slept and lived in a battlefield, a directionless, disorienting fog of violence.

There is an expression in Swahili, *vita ni mwizi*—war is a thief. The destruction of this place was brazen. Dead people lay in the streets. Shell-shocked neighbors stared at them. Bombs exploded in no discernible pattern. Children starved. All of my fears came true.

We all knew the routine: *If you hear an explosion, run as fast as you can, crawl under the bed, close your eyes, and pray to God.* We all learned every crack on the floor, every creak in each spring, where the wires that stuck out at the head of the bed could poke you in the eye.

One afternoon, I glanced at Estienne, one of Rob's cousin's children. He lay with me under the mattress, curled up and crying.

"Are we going to die?" he asked his sister, who lay with us too.

"No," she said. "None of us are going to die. We just need to pray for God to send angels to protect us."

I didn't believe in angels.

ONE DAY MAMA NEPELE SENT ME, and Dina, Mwasiti, and the other kids who lived in the house, to the pump. We needed water, we had no choice. She sent us together, in a group, to keep each other from making a minor but deadly mistake.

We walked twenty minutes, each of us with two twenty-liter yellow containers, and we arrived to find a dozen people in line arguing with a soldier who said he was closing the pump for the day. All of us needed to take our huge containers elsewhere.

So we backtracked and walked an hour up and over the hills down to a different valley by the lake. This one had a large house with running water. A guard outside the house told us that we needed to bring him rocks in exchange for filling our buckets. He pointed behind him to a large half-built stone cottage.

We combed the lakeshore, looking for big rocks. Mwasiti tied a huge one, the size of a large melon, behind her hip with her kitenge. She was now thirteen, well-muscled, confident as a racehorse in a paddock. You could see her strength was throttled down.

This was the only thing Mwasiti knew. This was her whole world. She had such pride, such defiant pride, like she'd been caught in a booby trap and was still standing in place saying there's nothing better than this. Her love of her home was unshakable. Patric, meanwhile, was five and still wanted to be babied. He picked a rock the size of a coconut and grimaced the whole way to the pump.

The soldier stared as we filled our jugs with water—mine only halfway. Then we started the long trek up the hill. By now it was afternoon. I carried my water on my head. We walked in silence. The streets were too quiet. The market was too quiet.

As the sun lowered I became too tired to keep up. I emptied a quarter of the water out of one jug, so that I could move faster. My whole body seized in a knot of fear right behind my backbone. It was getting dark. If we were out after 5:00 p.m., nobody would protect us.

The older women talked. I heard them talking about all

the things they do to women. I'd heard them say, *If you're a girl, someday you will have to be the sacrifice. The other girls will have to watch.*

A PRIEST LIVED NEXT DOOR to us, a white priest, and people from all over came to his house, hoping he would chase away the devil. The lines grew longer by the day, people screaming, crying, and fainting as they stood for hours in the equatorial sun. Some supplicants knocked on our door, asking for a bite to eat or a sip of water. We had so little.

One morning Mama Nepele woke up long before dawn and left the house before the curfew lifted to go stand in line at the mill. She hoped to beat the rush. After the sun rose we joined her, walking past the graveyard and through a tunnel.

Still we waited in line for hours. I wanted to leave my body. I hated that I had to eat. I hated my stomach, I hated my needs. The bargain my body offered did not feel worth it. I did not want the trouble anymore.

BACK HOME WE SPENT THE days under the bed or, really, taking turns under the bed because we didn't all fit. Claire's belly was as big as a three-kilo sack of rice and each time she fell asleep she had nightmares.

She saw people turning into animals, no doubt because, a few months earlier, rebels had taken over the house and hung a crocodile skin on the wall. Mama Nepele never dared to take it down. During the day military trucks rumbled down the streets, soldiers marching in small groups of six or eight, including pairs of little boys with guns they could barely hold.

The house sat partway up a small hill, a better location than on the main street. But still. All night the bombs exploded. People threw grenades. The adults pushed furniture against the windows. We moved the beds into the middle of the room. Yet my body felt as exposed as if I slept in a nightgown on a wide plateau. I felt cold even though the air was hot. I shook and could not stop.

Holding Mwasiti or Mado did not help. We all rattled and reeked with fear. Mama Nepele commanded us to be silent. We could not cry, so we did not cry. Noise provoked the devil.

THEN I WAS NOT JUST scared but sick. Malaria, depression, malnutrition, it did not matter. I could not stop sweating. I could not stop shivering. I couldn't eat.

Claire was too big and vulnerable to go out—a sadist's prize. Mama Nepele took me to the hospital.

None of my clothes fit. I was too skinny. I could not stand up. Mama Nepele wrapped me in a kitenge and tied my scrawny ten-year-old body to her back. I hated being carried. I didn't believe in its implicit promise of care and protection. But I was too weak to walk.

The war had no logic, no direction, no discernible objective, no face. It was everything, everywhere, all at once, and it stood for nothing at all. I was only semiconscious when we reached the hospital. Doctors prayed over me.

A nurse raised my head and made me drink charcoal, as Mucyechuru had done for Claire in Burundi. Nobody offered medicine.

We slept on a hospital bench. Then Mama Nepele carried me back home to die.

I WAS SO THIN. I was so weak. They had to hold me up to get me to the bathroom.

Mama Nepele lay down a mat under beautiful trees and she put me on it and read the Bible to me, to walk me through my own death. She knew I was going to die. Everybody knew I was going to die, and they all accepted that. But I thought, *I'm not going out like this. I'm not going to take this. I know where home is, I know where home is. I want to go home.*

MAYBE I NEEDED TO MOURN my old life. I recovered faster than anyone expected, and as soon as I was strong enough we left for Uvira. It was not better there. Flies swarmed the bodies in the street. One day Mama Nepele sent me and Mwasiti to walk up a steep hill near the edge of town to look for sweet potato leaves. The rocky hills scraped our knees. We found the vines stripped bare.

The Congolese government had started printing money. You now needed a whole plastic bag full of francs to buy charcoal, a suitcase full to buy sugar.

I prayed more. I sang more. I praised God.

I had this dream in which everyone was sleeping and I had to wake them up—wake them from their own near-deaths so that they might receive the word of God. When I was strong enough, I started doing lock-ins in churches, praying and kneeling all night behind a locked door, until my knees bled. I was obedient. I was holy. I cut my hair, nails, I wore long outfits, not showing any part of my body, like a nun. I regurgitated everything.

But once I fully recovered from my illness, I began to harbor doubts. There had always been preachers at the front gates of the refugee camps, greeting us with the message that we should focus on our lives beyond this one. This world was full of sinners, they said. We were those sinners. Our lives, this camp, they were hell, yes. But our true home was heaven.

Here, too, the preachers were saying that we were sinful. We should be punished. We should pray to God to make the suffering stop. I felt confused. We did not seem to be the sinners, not to me. We lacked food. We lacked water. People, not God, were causing us pain. Why should we be set on fire?

IN AUGUST, CLAIRE WENT TO the hospital to give birth to Freddy. The maternity nurses were so cruel. They said to all the women in labor, "Why did you spread your little legs? Why are you screaming and crying? Do you think you're the first to feel this kind of pain? Do you think you're the last?" They considered it their job to toughen women up.

The building was bombed five hours after Freddy was born. Claire did not have any clothes for him. She wrapped him in a hospital sheet and ran back to the house, and she joined us under the bed.

. . .

THE SHOOTING LASTED FOR DAYS. We pushed the beds into the hallways and lay under them there. Rob's mom snuck out to find water. We had nothing to eat, just a little sugar. Mama Nepele stirred the sugar into the water and gave it to Claire. "Drink, you need to drink," she said, "or you won't have milk for the baby. If you have no food, just water, you will poison yourself."

After a few days more, Mama Nepele begged a neighbor to give us a banana. Just one banana, for Claire.

We all stared at Claire and the baby. We prayed for Freddy not to cry. Time was a box, claustrophobic, no way out. We sang with no noise. We prayed with no faith. We peed on ourselves, and each of us pretended for the others not to see. The adults whispered:

"We need to leave."

"Where could we go?"

"To the lake and find a boat."

"Are you out of your mind? We will be caught. We will be killed."

"We are going to be killed anyway."

My brain stopped recording. I couldn't take it in. I prayed for tomorrow. That was my whole prayer: I prayed tomorrow would happen.

We are alive, we are lucky! We said that—it was absurd.

The only respite was dark humor, jokes about who should stand watch for whom while they defecated. The bathroom was behind the house. Who was quick, who was noisy, whose smell could draw fire.

When the guns were quiet we could hear the birds singing. We heard boots and men laughing. Freddy learned not to cry.

NO ONE WOULD LET THE children out, even on the days with little shooting—because all the adults knew. They knew people were the same. They knew we were scared and hungry, thus capable of becoming depraved.

The Congolese army was filled with war orphans, many close to my age, just eleven or twelve years old, children like me but who hadn't been forced to stay inside, under a bed; children who'd wandered out and met a man with a rifle who offered them candy or stew in exchange for passing forward their pain and spreading hate. We saw women with guns in the trucks too. Older girls.

Who was evil? The children who were hungry and scared? The men with guns offering them comfort and the means to feel purposeful and empowered?

If you're eleven and you haven't eaten, if you've been hiding all day and night and you are literally walking on spent artillery shells—and then someone shows you a nice house they've stolen and offers avocados and the stew they are cooking, you want it. I wanted it. I wanted release from misery, however ill-gotten and short-lived.

IN THE NORMAL WORLD, PEOPLE talk about shoes, people talk about love. We only talked about fire. Which machine gun made the loudest noise. Where the land mines were hidden. What bomb had just exploded, the name of it.

Boom baa cchshh ccshhh.

Mama Dina would wake up in the morning after a rain of fire and pray for us.

"Set the world straight for these kids!"

"It's going to be peaceful for you. All this sickness is going to be kicked away. You are going to walk strong."

That was the second or third breaking of everything, but the first rupture when I was old enough to understand just how cruel and terrible people can be without even knowing they are so cruel.

Life just kept shattering, the bricks of decency falling in a pattern both so illogical and so regular that we didn't even try to trace the chain reaction of destruction back to any particular origin anymore. There was pain. People felt threatened. Someone inflicted a wound.

EVERY NIGHT I HAD THE SAME DREAM.

I was on a massive boat, a fancy one, like a cruise ship, and we were so far out in the middle of the ocean that you couldn't see land. Everyone on board seemed happy. I was with Mariette.

Then, all of a sudden, the ship stopped and the electricity went off and everyone fell asleep, except me. I panicked and started trying to wake everybody. No, everyone was inert. The boat wasn't moving. All the lights had been cut. I ran around the deck in the pitch-dark, trying to find the captain. The dream went on for hours, or so I thought.

Then I heard a voice, a whisper, say, *Go to your backpack*. I went to my backpack and opened it. Inside was one of those mini Bibles like the ones the Congolese nuns gave us at my old horrible French school. As I pulled it out, the book transformed into a bigger and bigger Bible. As this happened, the ship started sinking. I found Claire and shook her violently, saying, "We're going to drown." Then the letters started flying off the Bible pages.

The ship lights came back on and everyone started waking slowly. None of the passengers had any clue what had happened. I said, frantic, to each one, "We almost sank! You almost died!" They all said, "No, we just fell asleep. It's late at night."

The dream was so upsetting. I refused to close my eyes for days. What if it came back again?

I told Claire my nightmare. "That is weird," she said. "Why would a giant ship sink?"

14

My mother used to test us. "Go get an orange," she'd say at the end of a meal, and then she'd cut the orange into pieces and watch us. There might be two pieces, there might be four pieces, there might be six pieces. She wanted to be sure we didn't take more than our share.

The exercise was illogical. We had trees full of oranges in the garden. We could each have our own orange. But if my mother didn't cut that one orange into enough pieces for everyone to share, the correct answer to the test was to cut it into more.

My mother was radical, in her actions if not her words. Sharing was her philosophy, an ideology to counter what she considered to be the emotionally stingy notions of possession or entitlement. We were never to think, *This orange is mine. I'm giving you what's mine.* We were to think, *This orange is ours. We're sharing what's ours.*

I think back to this often in trying to make sense of the world—how there are people who have so much and people who have so little, and how I fit in with them both. Often I find myself trying to bridge the two worlds, to show people, either the people with so much or the people with so little, that everything is yours and everything is not yours. I want to make people understand that boxing ourselves into tiny cubbies based on class, race, ethnicity, religion—anything, really—comes from a poverty of mind, a poverty of imagination. The world is dull and cruel when we isolate ourselves.

Survival, true survival of the body and soul, requires creativity, freedom of thought, collaboration. You might have time and I might have land. You might have ideas and I might have strength. You might have a tomato and I might have a knife. We need each other. We need to say: I honor the things that you respect and I value the things you cherish. I am not better than you. You are not better than me. Nobody is better than anybody else. Nobody is who you think they are at first glance. We need to see beyond the projections we cast onto each other. Each of us is so much grander, more nuanced, and more extraordinary than anybody thinks, including ourselves.

I've flown on private planes, I've lounged on private beaches. I've fallen asleep at night with no shelter, no parents, no country, no food. I've been made to feel worthless and disposable by the world.

I've seen enough to know that you can be a human with

a mountain of resources and you can be a human with nothing, and you can be a monster either way. Everywhere, and especially at both extremes, you can find monsters. It's at the extremes that people are most scared—scared of deprivation, on one end; and scared of their privilege, on the other. With privilege comes a nearly unavoidable egoism and so much shame, and often the coping mechanism is to give. This is great and necessary, but giving, as a framework, creates problems. *You give, I take; you take, I give—*both scenarios establish hierarchy. Both instill entitlement.

The only road to equality—a sense of common humanity; peace—is sharing, my mother's orange. When we share, you are not using your privilege to get me to line up behind you. When we share, you are not insisting on being my savior. Claire and I always looked for the sharers, the people who just said, "I have sugar, I have water. Let's share water. Let's not make charity about it."

THERE WAS ANOTHER LESSON MY mother taught me, this one with herbs. After she picked herbs from her garden she sorted her harvest: some herbs she hung to dry, some she buried, some she dried flat. She cooked with what needed to be used fresh. I think about that sorting now, too, as I try to untangle the pieces of myself, recognize and differentiate memories and emotions and place them them into categories I can use and understand.

When I first got to Hotchkiss, I was angry. I know that now but did not realize it then. I just felt guilty, sad, and ashamed.

Mrs. Thomas flew with me out to Connecticut, and on

the drive from the Hartford airport to Hotchkiss, I found myself trying to remember the landmarks: the big white church, the slopes of the hills. "This is a whole new chapter!" Mrs. Thomas said. "A new chapter in your life!"

She was steadfastly positive. But the truth is, as we drove onto the over-hundred-year-old estate of the campus, complete with boathouse, cemetery, and two hockey rinks, we both felt unmoored and confused. She'd done this: Mrs. Thomas's generosity had made Hotchkiss possible for me. She could not have hoped for a better outcome when she invited me into her home and tended to my schooling with such care.

Then my parents moved to Chicago and my world didn't move toward healing; it ruptured further. They arrived and I left to go to boarding school, something no one had foreseen.

I had a single room on the third floor of Wieler Dormitory. Mrs. Thomas opened the box of fresh bedding we'd ordered online—a pink, green, and white plaid print with green accent pillows—and made up my long twin bed. On the shelf above the radiator I placed framed pictures of me and my family with Oprah and Elie Wiesel. I could tell Mrs. Thomas was nervous for me. I had lived so many places, adapted so well, but I had never lived alone.

Mrs. Thomas cried when she left. I cried too. Then I napped and tried to get back into my toughest, most defended refugee mindset. I wanted, in my first walk across campus, to evince that I believed that this place had been waiting for me all my life.

I knew enough not to play the same game that the other students played. I didn't seek status. I figured there was more for me in being humble. If I told my math teacher that I didn't know how to do the problem set, she asked if anybody in class would be willing to meet with me. When I told my ethics professor I was confused, he said, "Let's meet for tea." We sat together in the dining hall. He approached me with such kindness and patience. We read Socrates and Plato two sentences at a time.

I was surrounded by teachers paid, not by me, to invest in my future. *Clemantine, are you doing all right? Clemantine, how's your project going?*

But I remained panicked. I could not stop moving.

Each morning I danced from 7:30 a.m. until my classes started at 9:00 a.m. This was not lovely or meditative. It was desperate, often aggressive. I was not kind to myself. I saw tutor after tutor, for hours each day. I managed the girls' field hockey team. I was drowning inside, and worse, I felt I had no right to be.

On weekends Claire would call and I would not pick up the phone. When I lived with the Thomases, I took care of her kids on weekends and babysat children in Kenilworth to earn money to buy them things. Now it felt like I did nothing. I had everything and I did nothing.

CHRISTMAS WAS AWFUL. THE OFFICIAL line in my family was: *We are so blessed. We are drenched in God's love.* But Claire's apartment was a war zone. My mother, my younger sisters, my brother, and my father all felt like one team. Claire and her children felt like another. Each squad huddled in a separate room to discuss plans, chores, it didn't seem to matter. This was a competition over whose needs got met. No one had let go of their sense of betrayal, not really. There was not a unified front.

I was unaffiliated. My younger sisters never talked to me. My brother never talked to me. I could not look at my father. Time had opened such a gap. You could scream, but the person on the other side was so far away that they couldn't hear you. I worried I had been selfish, going off to school. But my parents coming to the United States was supposed to be the big fix. Nothing was fixed.

Claire corralled almost the entire family into dressing up in red and black and holding glasses of sparkling cider so we could take perfect family New Year's pictures. But I could not. Mariette could not. She was now a teenager. Her fury was rude.

On New Year's Day, Mariette refused a direct request from my mother to help wash the dishes. I grabbed her arm and yanked her outside, onto the sidewalk.

"I don't care what you're going through," I yelled. "You cannot disrespect your elders. You're going to go inside and you're going to apologize to your grandmother."

"Nope," Mariette said. "That's not my grandmother. I don't even know her."

WHEN I RETURNED TO SCHOOL, to my single room with the pink-and-green duvet, I cracked. I had the skills to get into those long halls filled with portraits of pale, square-jawed men. I had the ability to work the system here. But none of that could protect me from my inner life. I was twenty and felt so old and so young. I'd always been alone but I'd never been alone. I was so many people and nobody at all.

One day, in a philosophy seminar, I sat around a mahogany table with my fellow students, the boys in sports jackets, the girls in sweaters, the winter sky sharp and crisp, the golf course in view. That day our class was focusing on war scenarios.

The professor, who'd been so patient with me, reading philosophy with me sentence by sentence in the dining room, had dedicated his life to teaching. He wore corduroys and ironed shirts over his comforting girth, and he kept a tight salt-and-pepper beard. That day he gave us a thought experiment: *You're a ferry captain with two passengers. Your boat is sinking. One passenger is old and one is young. Who do you save?*

With this, my veneer of decorum started to crumble. Before I arrived on campus I had asked the headmaster not to share my story. I didn't want to be a curiosity. Now I blurted out: "Do you want to know what that's really like? This is an abstract question to you?"

I packed myself together for a bit. Then, a few weeks later, around that same seminar table, the professor asked us all to share the presentations we'd prepared on whether or not to send troops into a Black Hawk Down–like war scenario—an extremely dangerous mission to capture warlords and their lieutenants, in a country like Somalia, filled with violence and starving children.

I hadn't prepared for the class. I knew I couldn't handle sitting in the library, using my intellect to take on war, chaos, and hunger as if those were abstract concepts, as if I'd never held Mariette on Lake Tanganyika, on a boat crammed with humans throwing heirlooms overboard. In class, as students went around the table, taking turns describing whether they'd intervene, I lost it, for real.

"You have no idea, do you?" I yelled as one girl spoke. "You've never been in that scenario. What gives you the right to even talk? This is real. That's me—and I have a name and I'm alive and there are people out there who are dead, or they're living but they're checked out and they hate the world because people in your country sat there and watched all of us getting slaughtered."

I ran out of class.

When I returned to fetch my bag, the professor asked me to meet him later in his office. I had loved that room— the drifts of papers and towers of books, the leather of his chair, soft and deep as his voice. As always, he spoke with patience and certainty. He told me that I needed to learn how to be a less emotional student.

"I can't be less emotional. It's personal," I said, all the while thinking, with cruelty, that I hadn't survived all that horror to sip tea and join his club.

My mind reeled with judgment. I believed that the professor's directive to me was meant to augment his own comfort while ignoring mine. It suited his need to exclude emotional episodes in class. They were unpredictable, not his speciality. He had no authority over feelings, no moral or intellectual high ground on that terrain. I dropped the seminar.

AFTER THAT, IN EVERY CLASS, even if the material had nothing to do with war, family, ethnicity, racism, poverty, I had to bring up my family, my childhood, my pain, and all my classmates would roll their eyes. Every paper I bent around my personal narrative. Every comment I made, every conclusion I drew, demanded that the teacher consider not my intellectual command of the material but my experience, me. They all tried to nudge me back toward the expected track, guide me into the Hotchkiss-approved form. The professor whose seminar I dropped was especially patient. He continued inviting me to his office and reiterating that my feelings were valid, no one was denying that, but in the classroom I needed to learn to channel them, not throw a tantrum, make everybody angry, and stomp away.

I couldn't do it. I wouldn't do it. I was unruly, full of contempt. I told them to go ahead and teach their students who knew nothing but comfort and were headed to careers at Goldman Sachs. I would not go along. I had not picked bugs out of my feet and watched my beaten sister nurse her baby while fleeing from one refugee camp to another to be lectured about human ethics by a man in corduroys.

Mrs. Thomas wanted me to call her every Sunday. I could not bear to talk to her. I could not bear to talk to Claire. I wanted only to broadcast, not converse. I had one friend, Luisa, and she sat with me in my room. She'd seen the pictures of my family with Oprah, me with Elie Wiesel, and she knew that I was suffering, but I still discussed almost nothing with her. I had so many nightmares. The nightmares of being trapped in the basement, the nightmares of the sleeping dead people on the boat. I was so lonely and depressed. I was in fifty pieces.

My advisor didn't know what to do with me. She called the dean at Yale, who did not know either. I was a special problem, a rare disease. I just wanted everyone to leave me alone. I could not handle myself, but I didn't want to be anybody's project.

My life, up until that point, had been so pragmatic and focused on survival. I sucked up all available data and synthesized the optimal persona for any given situation. What do you need me to wear? Who do you need me to be?

All that channeling I'd been doing . . . it had been an illusion. Now I crashed. No algorithm, no filter. I said whatever came to my mouth and didn't think twice. *This is just a different jungle,* I thought, *a different forest.*

I hated living by myself, for myself. It would have been easier if there were a locus for my anger: a single person. *You. You destroyed everything.* But there was no one person. No satisfying target. The world had torn and I thought I was bringing the pieces back together, but they just lay there, unsutured.

AT NIGHT, WHEN I COULDN'T sleep, I made bracelets. I'd done this since the ninth grade, when Mr. Thomas's mother moved into a retirement community. She was tough-minded and frugal, and over the decades she'd amassed a large tin full of buttons, beads, and single earrings. Mr. Thomas's mother decided she could finally part with the tin when we were cleaning out her old apartment. I brought it back to my bedroom. I saved everything too: nice plastic bags, glass bottles, ticket stubs.

So for hours, late at night, I sifted through the tin, picking out the ceramic beads and brass buttons, knotting and clustering them together on elastic string.

The bracelets I made were chunky and beautiful. I kept two for myself, then started giving them away to people who I could tell had been suffering, like a girl in my class who cut herself. I told the girl who cut herself that whenever she thought she deserved to feel pain, she should put on the bracelet and remember that she was special and loved.

Mrs. Thomas drove me to sewing stores to buy buttons by the pound. I also searched consignment shops, which I loved, with their leather shoes and abandoned housewares, the dozens of gold necklaces—each item deliberately relinquished.

I was trying to braid my story together, keep all my various lives connected. I decided to make a hundred bracelets and give them all away. With each one I would let go of something painful or destructive in myself. With the first bracelet, I gave up Coke. I'd been drinking two cans a day for the caffeine. I was punishing myself, assuaging my guilt over surviving, with lack of sleep.

Next I tried to let go of hating my legs. I hated my scars—the one on my thigh from a barbed-wire fence and the one on my calf from the major infection I'd contracted at age eleven that ate a hole in my flesh.

It wasn't working. I needed something more.

A professor's wife invited me over to their house sometimes. Perhaps she saw the isolation in my eyes. She sewed and I liked the noise of her machine, so I decided, as an art project, to make a dress. At first I imagined one made of tulle, with a long papier-mâché train. But fabric was more expensive than I realized, so I settled on working with canvas from the art room.

The pattern I chose was for a one-shoulder dress with a

fitted bodice, a wide belt, a large fabric flower sewn like a brooch on the left collarbone, and an A-line skirt. I draped it on the mannequin. It looked so white and pure. So I decided to paint it red. I brought the dress to the art room and started mixing colors. Beet, ladybug, stop sign. I couldn't find the right red. Finally I felt satisfied, watered down my paint, and took the dress outside.

I lay it on a sheet of plastic on the ground, filled up a brush, and splattered. The paint now looked exactly like blood. I kept splattering, a massacre, trying to let go of my pain. The belt I painted entirely. It looked like a gash, open flesh. I displayed the dress, back on the mannequin, in the year-end art show. I titled the work *Drop Dead Gorgeous*. It did look pretty if you weren't paying attention.

Everybody passed it and said, "Clemantine, what a beautiful dress."

15

I sat with Freddy and Mariette and our torn luggage. People kept passing us, either sneering or averting their eyes, saying nothing. We'd arrived in Zambia. We were invisible.

Around the edges of the outdoor market in Lusaka ran open gutters. The filthy ground had been drenched with rain two or three days before. You could see footprints baked into the earth where the sun hit the ground directly, and a sludge of mud, thick as quicksand, drew flies in the shade. What had been clean, pure rainwater just days before was now a putrid medium for waste—fish carcasses, rotten vegetables, excrement, plastic bags. A young man dipped a bucket in the gutter and pulled it back out, full, to wash a bike.

After leaving Zaire, we'd tried to get back to Rwanda through Burundi, but it was too dangerous. So we retreated to Tanzania, again, as we had the last time we'd fled Zaire. Claire and I both wanted to make it to back to South Africa now. But that was too dangerous with a baby and a toddler, so a priest helped put us on a boat to Zambia. We'd taken four buses to get here and arrived with no plan.

So Claire left us at the teaming COMESA market while she walked off to find, or try to find, shelter and food. Claire refused to go back to a refugee camp. She was done with that life. Done with waiting hours in line for the toilet; done with eating only beans; done with living for a year in a plastic bag that someone else called a tent.

We sat for what felt like hours. Time passed, we did not move. Each stall was crammed with cheap pots, plastic sandals, blouses, kitenges, sleeping mats, toothbrushes, jeans, soap, underwear, bras, umbrellas, electric stoves—the full kit of consumer goods required for the cheapest form of urban life.

Between the stalls, in the center aisle, were stacks of wooden pallets, less desirable commercial real estate than the stalls, as you had to cover your goods with plastic sheeting every time it rained, and these pallets were topped with still more cheap pots, plastic sandals, blouses, kitenges, sleeping mats, toothbrushes, jeans, soap, underwear, bras, umbrellas, electric stoves.

By noon the market was thick with Zambian women in kitenges, flip-flops, and T-shirts, many of them bargaining and screaming at each other, most looking exhausted, the kind of dull-eyed chronic tiredness that comes from the nonstop stress of being broke. Car horns barked, music blared—it was so chaotic and loud.

Children, many of them my age, stood on the edges of

the market, begging for money or food. I was so hungry and so scared. I could not stop thinking about *ugali,* rice, groundnuts, bananas, avocados—anything to put in my mouth.

I was new at being alone with both kids but also knew I could not broadcast my insecurity, so I kept my eyes down. I felt so self-conscious—a ten-year-old with a toddler and a baby. Who did people think we were? Freddy slept through the noise, which made me feel grateful but also mystified. He looked so shiny and perfect, his dark skin black and lacquered like a beetle.

Mariette, meanwhile, now three, sat by my side, crying. She too was hungry and scared, but I could not comfort her. I could not engage or I'd disintegrate myself. We had nowhere to go, no home in the world—no money, no friends, no relatives.

FINALLY A WOMAN STOPPED IN front of me and spoke to me gently in a language I did not understand. She then pulled out of her bag two little plastic sacks of cold water. She handed one to me and one to Mariette. We drank like thieves. The woman spoke again. I shook my head and said in Swahili, "Thank you but I do not understand."

This time she responded in Swahili. She asked me if I'd like to sit with her in her stall in the shade.

So we sat there. More time passed. I felt slightly better, less like carrion, less forgotten and exposed. But still time didn't matter. Our lives had no value and therefore there was no relevance to how our hours were spent.

Claire returned with mixed news. A woman had given

her the address of her pastor and said we should go to his house and knock.

So we walked down a long flat street, away from the chaotic bus depot, away from the COMESA market, out of the city proper, on paved but potholed roads. Both shoulders were filled with hundreds of people walking, skinny black people with excellent posture and inspired outfits built of secondhand clothes walking slow and steady, the gait of people who walked for miles.

The pastor's wife answered the door. She'd been cleaning—she had a mop in her hand and a blue-and-gold kitenge wrapped on her head. Claire apologized for the inconvenience and for needing to ask a favor, but here we were, she explained, herself, her two young children, and her little sister, and we had nowhere to sleep.

The pastor's wife, God bless her, paused only for a moment before inviting us in. She gave us food and water and pointed to some rolled cotton mats that we could use to sleep on, on her swept floor.

The pastor, when he returned, looked at us with soft, weary eyes. Two days later, he helped us buy bus tickets to Mozambique. He thought perhaps we could, and should, backtrack to South Africa, where Rob still lived and we'd had better luck.

The ride was so long, twelve hours long. When we arrived at the border, immigration would not let us through. We had no visa, no home. So we rode the twelve hours back to Lusaka and once again walked along the shoulder of the long flat road to the pastor's house.

We knew the pastor's wife didn't want us to return, and Claire regretted the inconvenience, but she felt it was not unreasonable to ask. We were people—homeless, poor, countryless, vulnerable people. Kindness was a Christian commandment—we could ask for a roof and food.

The pastor's wife opened the door and loudly sighed and invited us back in. She tolerated our presence for two weeks. Then she said her mother-in-law was coming to visit and we needed to move out.

AGAIN WE WALKED, FREDDY TIED to my back, Mariette tied to Claire's. We walked past the roadside shacks selling fruit, T-shirts, oil, maize, and bicycle tires, our faces impassive, or at least Claire's was. Some guys called out to her in Kinyarwanda, "Hey, beautiful!" Male attention was a liability more than a help, but since they'd catcalled her in Kinyarwanda, she stopped.

"You from Rwanda?" Claire asked.

One of the men was very tall. The tall man said yes.

"My name is Claire," she said, and the taller man's face contorted and he started crying.

His sister had died in the genocide, he said. Her name had been Claire too.

Claire said, "I'm so sorry." What else was there to say? Claire then explained our situation. "I have nowhere to sleep. I'm with my younger sister and two kids—I don't care if you put me in the kitchen or whatever."

The man with the sister named Claire invited us to come to his apartment to sleep. His friend, who lived with him, tried to stop it. "I have a girlfriend," he said, his voice clipped. "We can't take you . . ."

Claire just stood there and repeated herself. "I have two

kids—I don't care if you put me in the kitchen or whatever."

The man with the sister named Claire told us to follow him to his sweet potato stand. When we got there, the friend broke down. He said, "I think I remember you from a church dance."

WE MOVED IN WITH THE tall man and his friend. Claire scrambled to make money to help our hosts with food and rent. She now spoke so many languages. She befriended everybody, greeted everybody. "Hey, Auntie! Hey, Uncle!" she called out to all the neighbors, always with a smile. She would not be broken. I resented her leaving me with the kids, but she remained an immovable force, determined to hold on to a shard of independence and not to be pitied.

She was also never willing to sell her body, which I was now old enough to realize was a miracle. I did not judge the other women and girls around me, who wore too much makeup and heels to advertise their trade—they had nothing and needed to survive. But my mother had been adamant about never, ever trading on sex.

I thought back to those lessons my mother casually imparted to Claire, when we all stood in the kitchen and our mother talked in her Catholic way about how special it is to be a woman and how when you sleep with a man he takes something from you. He knows you inside and out and you can never get your whole self back.

Claire tried so hard to hold on. Or maybe it wasn't trying exactly; she refused to let go of her sense of self-worth.

So many women in the market spent their minuscule

profits on lotion to lighten their skin. The world made them feel ugly. Men made them feel ugly. They wanted to feel beautiful.

A FEW WEEKS LATER, ROB unexpectedly showed up. He'd taken a bus to Lusaka and asked around until he found us. He arrived with nothing, no toy for Mariette and no money to help feed and clothe his new son, whom he'd never met. Claire felt too embarrassed to continue living at the Rwandan men's house, for them to see how Rob treated her.

Lusaka was such a divided city. As I now knew from our bus rides, the wealthy lived in splendor in large homes with pools and lawns. The well-off lived nicely too, on their paved roads, behind their gates.

The merely poor lived in tiny tin-roofed cottages in dusty neighborhoods. They had no indoor plumbing, and their children had to walk an hour to get to school, but they carefully tended the bougainvillea vines blooming by their front doors, and the tomatoes, beans, and greens in their gardens, and they built nice, dignified lives. Farther out still were neighborhoods of half-built houses, rebar sticking out of cement like arms waving for help.

Then there was Chibolya, the slum we moved into. I'd come to believe that there were stages of death, that you don't just fall down and die. The market that first day, feeling invisible while Claire tried to find us a place to stay that night—that was one level of death. Chibolya was far beneath that. Along with filthy rain gutters and pools of standing water, it had open garbage dumps; children with no shoes and torn clothes sitting expressionless in the dirty street; crumbling cinder-block houses; girls blatantly selling themselves; kids pressing their bodies into the doorways of schools which their parents had not paid for them to attend, hoping, against reason, that the teachers would feed them lunch.

We rented the smallest possible room, just five by ten feet. Even apart from its size, the place felt suffocating, as though we'd passed through a one-way valve into a level of death so deep that I wanted to tear off my skin to remind myself I was still alive.

Our room faced a courtyard. In that courtyard, on a stool, sat one of the landlady's daughters, making sure that we did not use the shower in the communal bathroom, as we had not paid for that right.

When it rained, the garbage dumps swelled, the trash inflating like a grotesque quilted leviathan. Each raindrop on the tin roof sounded like a footfall in a deafening stampede. Our kitchen consisted of one ancient electric stove with wires sticking out from the heating coils. It sparked when you turned it on. I was terrified of being electrocuted. I wore plastic shoes while I cooked.

CLAIRE'S HUSTLE WAS IN THE MARKET. She befriended a woman who rented a spot on the open-air wooden pallets. The woman sold underwear and bras, black, white, and red. She let Claire share her table. Claire still said hello to everybody. She helped bring in business. If a customer purchased from Claire's side of the table, the woman who paid the table's rent let Claire keep the profit—Claire's presence was still a net plus.

Soon other merchants were bringing Claire commissions—jeans, soccer jerseys. They'd give her a button-down shirt and say, "I need thirteen dollars back." All the market would be selling the exact same shirt for $15. Claire would sell it for $14.50.

A little money today was better than no money at all—that was Claire's reasoning. Soon Claire had more commissions than she could handle. She returned the unsold merchandise to its owners at the end of the day. She did not want to be responsible. In Chibolya, things got stolen.

My hustle was getting through the day. How to claim dignity. How to keep the kids clean—in particular, how to keep Freddy from crawling in the filth. How to roll up my sleeping mat. How to "shine" the house, which was really just dousing the floor with petrol to keep out the bugs. How to wash my loud, floral, short-sleeved Hawaiian shirt, which I loved and which I wore with my jean skirt, tied at the waist. How to make the kids cute, and thus make them lovable and seen. How to buy the cheapest vegetables, the nearly rotten tomatoes, sweet potatoes, beans, and spinach, go home, put on my plastic sandals, and make a stew.

The kids needed so much. I would not allow Mariette to play with friends. She got too dirty that way. Everybody thought Freddy's big belly was so cute. It was not cute. I was the most tired eleven-year-old in the world.

There was no infrastructure really. The water pump was a twenty-minute walk away. To go with Freddy and Mariette, I needed to borrow a wheelbarrow, although borrowing a wheelbarrow meant that I needed to return it to its owner with an extra gallon or two of water.

My body was changing, which was terrifying. In the

water line I heard the women talking about whose husband was cheating with whom. Rob cheated, all the men cheated. They needed to feel better than somebody, and the easiest people to feel better than were their wives.

I was such easy prey for a man with something to prove. I was nobody—an eleven-year-old girl who belonged to nobody. I did not stand in the water line after 4:00 p.m. for fear of being raped. Even earlier in the day, I tried to do what I had done since age seven. I tried to puff myself up and make myself bigger, 100 feet tall and 150 years old.

But sometimes it felt harder than ever. Claire and I had already had five types of lives and we'd built nothing. I shot down every conversation. I trusted nobody.

One day, in the line at the water pump, Mariette ran off and I left my jugs and wheelbarrow in my place while I chased her. When I returned, my water jugs and wheelbarrow had been moved to the side, to eliminate my place in line. The women kept talking, gossiping—whose husband was cheating on who—but I could no longer hear them.

I kept thinking, *I can't listen, because if I listen I will kill myself. Staying alive is too hard if you end up like this.*

INSIDE THE COMPOUND I DID have one friend, Rhoda. Her mother was our landlady. Her younger sister was Joy, the self-appointed policewoman of the shared bathroom. Together they lived in an apartment with several rooms at the corner of the compound near the gate, and they were fat, which everybody envied. Fat meant you ate three meals a day. Fat meant you rode the bus instead of walking endless miles.

Rhoda was a couple years older than me, tall and light-skinned, with thick, beautiful black curls and a hideous white skirt with floral embroidery that she loved. She lazed around, chewing on her tongue, the tip of it hanging out of the side of her mouth like the tab on a can of soda.

Her laziness was not slothful. Her laziness was relaxed. She was languid with the certainty that she did not need to hustle. Life would take care of itself. After she ate cereal, she put her spoon down exactly where she'd finished and walked away. She dropped her dirty clothes and left them on the floor. Someone else would clean up.

Despite living here, in Chibolya, Rhoda's mother in-stilled in her children a sense that their world was perfect, and it was, compared to mine. They ate meat. They traveled to visit family in Livingstone, Zambia, near Victoria Falls. They attended school. Rhoda was too lazy to study, but she let me touch her notebooks. I still had my pencil case with my name on it. I would have gone to school in Rhoda's place if I thought I could have passed for her.

FOR THIRTY MINUTES A DAY, the sunlight hit our one window just so and the glass became a mirror. I was drawn to the mirror but also repulsed. In the reflection I saw my aunt. I saw my mother, but my mother's hair was always down, wavy and luminescent. Mine was an ugly, self-braided mess.

A boy began coming around. He was fifteen and lanky, and when he dropped by he brought candy for Claire's kids. I wanted no part of him. Within a few months of living in Chibolya, Rob had a girlfriend he made no effort to hide and was back to beating Claire. If Claire complained about anything—eating once a day, living in one room—Rob said, "Go back to Rwanda! Do you even have any family there?"

IMMIGRATION STARTED CRACKING DOWN. About six months after we arrived in Zambia, Claire quit going to the market because people without papers were being thrown in jail.

Rob got caught by immigration police. He was reckless about seeing his girlfriend. A soldier stopped him one night on the way home from her house. He had no visa, so he got thrown in jail. I thought Claire might disown him. Rob probably hoped she would.

A woman we met on the bus invited us over on Sundays and let us watch TV. She had an abusive husband too, and she advised Claire to stick it out. He'd shape up when the kids were older, the woman told Claire. He'd want Mariette and Freddy to love him so he'd stop beating on her.

So most mornings Claire packed up *ugali* and stew, if we had any, and walked the seven miles to bring it to Rob in jail. While there, she made a point of lingering at the door of the prison director's office, asking him, "How was your lunch? How was your tea today?" After she'd exchanged niceties with the prison director half a dozen times, she said, "I'm not leaving until you hear my story." She lied and told him that Rob was the breadwinner. He sold clothes in the market. We needed him to feed the family. Immigration made exceptions for parents with small businesses.

The director released Rob the next day.

. . .

CLAIRE'S DEDICATION TO ROB DIDN'T help her. When he returned from prison his behavior was worse than ever. All the women in the compound were afraid of him, though the truth is almost all the women were afraid of almost all of the men.

Women were used to the idea that they would suffer, that they would feel low. For the men, it was hard to reconcile their expectations and ideas about masculinity with this life. As a result, they overcompensated with wild displays of rage, open affairs.

We were so poor that we didn't even have full bathroom privileges, just the toilet. Rhoda's sister, Joy, complained if we had guests over too frequently and they used the bathroom too much.

One night Rob came home angry and beat up Claire. It was very late, almost 11:00 p.m., and when he finished he screamed, "Take your kids and get out!" Chibolya started closing down at dusk and was terrifying in the dark. So much desperation, so many bodies packed so close together.

Still, Claire immediately picked up Mariette and I picked up Freddy, and we hid outside the courtyard gate in the bushes. We could not leave the kids with him. We did not want him to find us.

I felt ready to be evil. I wanted to break a window and attack Rob with shards of glass. I wanted to break my whole world. I had so much anger at Claire built up. I hadn't asked to parent these kids. I hadn't asked for all the moving. Claire now had bruises everywhere. Crouched and shaking, she tried to reassure me, as if I, too, was a small child. "Don't worry," she said. "We'll figure it out . . ." I could not take it.

"That man just kicked us out of the house that *you* paid

for, that you paid for by going to the market every day to bring home money and food for the kids and for me." I had never said anything before that acknowledged what she'd done for me. I had never acknowledged her strength. I was desperate for her to recognize mine. "We need to take care of our kids, our beautiful kids," I said. *Our* kids, not just her kids. Not his kids. Our kids, Claire's and mine.

We stayed there, in the bushes, for an hour. Then we snuck back into the compound and knocked on the door of an older woman. She let us in for the night.

A WEEK LATER CLAIRE BROUGHT me and the kids to live with another family on the edge of Lusaka, in a modest neighborhood of tiny stand-alone houses with tin roofs. Claire was scared. We were eating once a day. The home belonged to a first cousin of the woman who invited us over on Sundays. The cousin, too, had left Rwanda generations ago. She wore long house dresses and offered to take me and Claire's children in. I loved her hands, her long nails painted red, her skin hennaed from knuckles to wrist. I sat in her kitchen for hours and watched her cook. She chopped, peeled, and stirred with precision. She never chipped her nails.

Every day, in her kitchen, she followed the same pattern: First she cooked all the starches, then all the vegetables, then the fish. When she finished, she made *mandazi*. She rolled them in extra sugar, or extra cinnamon, or chai spices—whatever Freddy or Mariette requested.

"Clemantine, I'm going to braid your hair," she said. "Come here, sweet girl."

"Clemantine, we're hungry. What are we hungry for?"

My body kept filling out. So she took me shopping. We bought a crinkly black dress, knee length, short sleeved, with tiny purple, pink, and white flowers. It dried fast in the sun. I loved it because it fit.

CLAIRE MADE MONEY SENDING FAXES for a while. She met an official at the Belgian consulate by walking into the office one day and pretending she was there to sell a necklace to his secretary. Once inside, she charmed the man into letting her use his fax machine to try to learn about our parents. From there it was an easy hustle to start sending faxes for neighbors, for a profit.

By then it was safe to return to selling in the market. She sold bras, underwear, and shirts on commission, and she also met a woman who was part of a UN group providing refugees with microloans to start small businesses. Claire applied, still the A student, still the Canadian anthem singer, not waiting to be saved by anybody but herself. When the woman heard Claire's story, she said, "I'll be your aunt or whatever you want to call me!"

When Claire made a little more money, Mariette, Freddy, and I returned to living in Chibolya, with Rob. Every day, at 4:00 p.m., I dressed up and walked around the block with the kids, all of us clean. Sometimes I did an errand, like buy salt. It didn't matter. That was not the point. The point was to be seen in the world.

I wanted to say, *I am here. I need you to see me, I need you to see that I am here. You, world, cannot make me crumble. I am alive, I am alive, I am alive.* I wanted everybody to turn, stare, and say, "Oh my goodness, look at that beautiful dress. Who do we have here?" I needed to tell myself, every day, *I exist. I am bathed, my hair is washed. My clothes are ironed. I am taking care of these kids. These kids are clean. I, too, am clean.*

For that one hour, I felt proud. Not just dignified but certain, impermeable, a rock. The sun that turned the window glass into a mirror had confirmed my existence. But I needed to see my body—I needed to own it.

Almost every other minute of my existence, I felt the pain of being nobody's child, the sting of the assumptions people make when you don't have a mother and you don't have a father. People assume you're adrift, in play. They assume that you are vulnerable. They assume your needs are lesser, that your will is broken, that your body can be bent to theirs.

But clean, in that dress, holding Mariette and Freddy's hands, I felt like somebody's somebody. I whispered to myself the words I needed to hear. "Beautiful girl, sweet sweet girl, look at how the dress fits you."

Back in the compound I took it off. I started dinner with the terrifying stove. By the time Claire came home, I had returned to being a maid.

CLAIRE CAME HOME ONE DAY with news. The UN woman—the one who gave microloans and whose house Claire prayed at—told Claire that the UN had launched a program for refugees who'd survived genocide to gain entry to the United States. The United States, to Claire, was the ultimate land of hustling and rewards. You could start a business and grow rich. You could have six cars. You could have a faucet with beer on tap. When you landed, somebody would take your hand and give you everything. They would buy you shoes. They would buy a house. You would have a phone. Would Claire like to apply? the friend asked.

The following day Claire dressed in her jeans, boots, and crisp white blouse and walked to the American embassy. The UN woman met Claire there and helped her fill out the English forms. Among the information requested was a list of family members. Claire included Rob's name.

The woman scoffed. "Claire, that's very stupid."

Claire had told her about Rob. His cheating had become even more brazen. His girlfriend, a woman in her early forties, came by in heels and bright lipstick to pick up Rob at our house. She often carried department store shopping bags. If Claire told her to stay away, she spit. "What can you do about it? I can report you to immigration."

Yet Claire was unwavering. "If God gives us all the opportunity, we need to take it. What will I tell my kids? Maybe he will change when we get to America."

THREE MONTHS LATER, CLAIRE RECEIVED news that she had been called in for an interview. The interview was on a Monday. She told Rob the Friday night before. "You're going to America?" he said. "You don't care about anyone in Africa? You don't have anyone in your life?"

Claire was impassive. "If you want to go, go. If not, I will go with Clemantine and the kids."

That weekend, for the first and only time, Rob ironed Claire's clothes. On Monday we all dressed up: me in my black dress, Claire in her jeans and crisp white shirt. Rob shined his shoes. I braided Mariette's hair. Freddy kept his shirt tucked in over his belly.

I had never been to the part of Lusaka with the embassies. It was a giant garden filled with tall trees, manicured and clean. In the embassy we waited in silence in a long line. I hated lines. Nobody spoke. When the clerk called us, he asked Claire about our lives, about leaving Rwanda. I didn't listen.

On the way out the clerk whispered to Claire, "You passed. I should not tell you this, but you passed. Don't tell anybody."

NOW I HAD THIS SECRET, this glistening, gorgeous secret that I turned over like a marble in my mind. We were going to America, land of *The Jetsons* and *Zoom*. Claire promised that when you land, straightaway they buy you shoes. Everybody becomes rich. The country was inviting us. We would belong. When you don't belong to a country, the world decides that you don't deserve a thing.

We started deep-cleaning our house. Claire bought us new clothes. Our puffy jackets. Plus brand-new white Keds sneakers, a maroon shirt with a white stripe on the collar, and skinny jeans for me; OshKosh overalls and a flowered shirt for Mariette; a blue-and-gray-striped shirt and jeans for Freddy.

The night before we left, Claire gave our pots and

bedrolls to the older woman who'd taken us in when Rob kicked us out of the house.

We rode a bus to the airport.

I cried the entire flight to Chicago. No one would find us now.

16

Years after that first show, when I was twenty-three and a junior in college, Oprah called to say that she wanted to fly me and Claire, first class, to South Africa, to attend an event at her new high school, the Oprah Winfrey Leadership Academy for Girls, just south of Johannesburg.

The school was a fantasy—wide lawns, stucco buildings inlaid with traditional basket patterns, frescoed murals of girls dancing. Oprah spoke and then I spoke, and after that Oprah squeezed my hand and said, "My girl, my girl, my girl."

I wore a green chiffon dress, the same shade of green as the girls' school uniforms. After the event we took pictures. I noticed, in the school's front lobby, three dolls, one small, one medium, one large, all beaded from head to toe, all with round red eyes.

"Did I have a doll with beads?" I asked Claire. In my conscious mind I'd forgotten about the story Mukamana had told me.

Claire had no patience for these questions. "No, you did not have a doll with beads."

"Why do I remember a doll with beads?" I asked.

"It's that story. You were always asking me to tell you."

Claire then walked off, shutting down that conversation for the day.

The following morning we returned to the school. Again I stared at the dolls.

"Can you please tell me that story?" I asked Claire. She looked exasperated with me. I hated that expression. I'd seen it ten thousand times. The expression said, *Don't push me. I don't need you. You are a negative drag.*

"Remember?" she finally deigned to say. "There was a girl who smiled beads . . ."

That was enough. The story came rushing back. It now made sense: my bracelets, all my beads.

The traditional Rwandan fable starts with a barren mother. She's miserable and desperate for a baby, as every other woman in her village has a child. When she walks down into the valley, to fetch water, she prays for a child, and while she's praying, the rains come in.

The water comes down and the thunder roars but still the woman keeps praying. She wants a child to love now, and to care for her later, when she grows old. The thunder rattles louder, and the woman prays louder still, louder than the thunder itself.

"Who is the woman whose cries are louder than mine?" the thunder demands. "You. You must stop."

The woman refuses. The thunder demands again and grows irate. So the mother offers the thunder a bargain: she'll quiet her prayers if the thunder gives her a child. The thunder agrees.

Months later, the woman gives birth to a beautiful baby, the most beautiful girl in the village, the most beautiful girl she's ever seen. The baby is part thunder, and therefore part magic, and her smile is so bright that whenever it crosses her lips, out flows a gorgeous trail of beads. The mother is filled with pride and jealousy, and feels terrified that her daughter will be stolen, so she locks her in the house. Yet one day, when the mother goes to the market, she forgets to lock the door. The girl who smiles beads walks out and disappears.

The mother searches everywhere, through her whole village, over the next hill, all through the night. She asks neighbors and strangers if they've seen her girl and they all say yes. The beads, they say, they saw her beads just this morning. Not her body, just her glittering contrail. They looked for her, they wanted to see her, but she was always gone.

The thunder, hearing that his daughter is lost, comes down from the sky to find her. He lines up all the girls on all the hills and makes them smile on command. When he finds the girl who smiles beads, he takes her back with him to his home in the sky. Her mother returns to crying—she is childless again.

When my nanny Mukamana told me the story, she just set up the character and the premise and let me fill in the pieces. "And what do you think happened next?" she said. I loved this question. It was such a gift. Whatever my answer, whatever plot I chose, Mukamana told me I was correct. In this way, the girl who smiled beads became the answer to all puzzles, a way to give shape to a world that my parents would not explain and later Claire would not explain, a means to bend and mold reality that I could grasp and accept. I thought I was the girl. I thought the beads were fire, though sometimes I thought the beads were water or time. In my version of the story, the girl walks the earth and she is always safe, there but not there, one step ahead. And she is truly special, undeniably strong and brave—a dream, a superstar, a goddess of sorts. I needed to believe those things were possible and that they might be true about me too. In the narrative the world proffered, I was nothing. The world told me I was nothing. The plot provided by the universe was filled with starvation, war, and rape. I would not—could not—live in that tale.

Instead, I would be the girl who smiled beads, my version of the girl who smiled beads, one who had power and agency over her life, one who did not get caught. I already had the boxes of buttons and beads, all my *katundu,* my stuff. When I told the girl's story, when I imagined and determined the future, I told it this way: *Not that long ago, in a land full of hills, not that far away, there was a beautiful girl, a special, glowing, magical girl who smiled beads. She traveled and she left them in her wake, like fairy dust, and by the time anyone tried to catch her, she was gone.*

MY ROOMMATE AT YALE ARRIVED on Old Campus before I did, with her blue IKEA couch and potted houseplants, and she took the bottom mattress on the bunk bed, leaving me the top. Everything she owned was soft, matching, and in order. I'd shipped my jumble of boxes, my *katundu,* to New Haven straight from Hotchkiss. I wished our room was bigger, but I was relieved that it was clean. The week before, I'd attended a pre-orientation camp with two hundred other incoming freshmen, out in the middle of Connecticut somewhere, in the woods. We played bonding games and square-danced in a barn and it was fun enough, I supposed. But the hamburgers weren't cooked through, the cabins smelled like urine, and the mattresses were hard and green. I kept imagining what Claire would think if she saw it. *You guys are all smart enough to get into Yale and dumb enough to stay in a place like this?*

Still, I got a Yale sweatshirt, I wore J.Crew. Sunday through Wednesday I sat in Sterling Library, in the sunken leather chairs, reading until 4:00 a.m., and for the next three nights I went out, attending house parties and dancing in the sticky, grabby scene at a bar called Toad's Place. But it was distraction, not connection; losing, not finding myself. I knew the preppy conservatism of Kenilworth and Hotchkiss could never represent me. But I was not like Claire either, still enjoying her Nigerian soap operas, still wearing kitenges and cooking *ugali.* Claire's house was filled with Africans—Nigerians, Congolese, Rwandans, most notably my parents, nieces, nephew, and siblings. I wanted nothing to do with it.

I DECIDED NOT TO GO home the summer after my first year at Yale. I signed up for a Yale trip to Kenya to study Swahili. I convinced myself it would be lovely. I would wander out into the wider world, start connecting the dots of my life, not stay trapped inside these new pretty, cloistered walls.

I had a boyfriend, Zach, who wanted to go to Kenya too. Zach was perfect—handsome, confident, sparkling, a junior from Atlanta, half Nigerian, half Dutch. He was in my Swahili class and he learned Kinyarwanda to speak to me—me, the girl who asked questions as a young child that nobody would ever answer. It felt like the most romantic thing in the world.

Together in Kenya, I told myself, we'd be in a beautiful place. We'd eat great food. I'd be accepted, understood, praised, even embraced. The Kenyans would approach me, saying, "Oh, wow, you know our languages—how amazing is that?"

Before we left, the Yale language department issued a dress code. Women, the university said, needed to respect local customs and not wear shorts, short skirts, or spaghetti straps. We needed to pack scarves to wrap our heads and bodies.

I did not feel obligated to obey. I was different, or so I believed, a special native daughter returning to my continent, not as a socially worthless refugee but as a United States citizen, a Yale student no less. I had an American passport. I had a certifiably valuable identity.

My worth was now an intrinsic part of my being. My power could not be stolen from me.

THAT SPRING, ZACH AND I hung out at the Afro-American Cultural Center. The place was filled with fabulous black people. Black Europeans. Black Jamaicans. Black Haitians.

Black Americans. Black Africans. I had not been around so many black people since I left Zambia.

I'd built so little connection to black beauty. I'd studied slavery and the abolition of slavery. I'd studied Harriet Tubman and Martin Luther King Jr. Yes, I knew and loved Toni Morrison, James Baldwin, and Maya Angelou. I had memorized every word of "Still I Rise," and each stanza was a mantra.

Did you want to see me broken?
Bowed head and lowered eyes?
. . . .
You may kill me with your hatefulness,
But still, like air, I'll rise.

But Angelou's pain was not my pain. The slave story, while I related to it, was not my story. White America had not caused my wounds.

I had known so few elegant, educated, ambitious, cultured black men. The men around Claire's house were so decimated inside that I wondered if even they knew the true source of their pain. My father had given up. Rob had suffered more than he could absorb and violence leaked from his skin.

Zach, charming Zach, was a revelation. One night he took me to New York City to see Alvin Ailey's dance troupe.

Another night, at the Afro-American house, a woman from Senegal stood up and recited a poem in Wolof, then in English. I was mesmerized—the way she dressed, her eyes, her black lips, her command of her native language, her command of herself. I wanted that wholeness, that coherence. I wanted to be her. But I could not gather myself up, not even here.

Before long I was instigating debates about the less seemly parts of African culture. I lectured my fellow students at the house about my time living among the women in Malawi, who dropped to the ground when a man entered a space. The women in Zambia taught to roll on the floor after their husbands had sex with them, to express their subservience and gratitude. The Rwandan children beaten before school and their parents calling those beatings *kiboko*, breakfast.

People grew angry, defensive, and annoyed. My narrative was counterproductive, they said, a white man's view of the African mess. Many of those students had parents who'd sent them to boarding school in England to study, or at least had parents financially stable enough to send them to twelve years of school. I did not want to hear their views of Africa the beautiful.

Zach pulled me aside. "Clemantine, you're very abrupt and not letting people have room to comment . . ."

But I was done, gone. "No, no, no," I said. "This is real. People kill each other. We do that to each other. And ourselves."

I FELT THE UGLINESS THE moment we landed in Mombasa.

We took a cab to our boarding house, which was hideous, and sure enough, just a twenty-minute walk toward the shore stood Fort Jesus, a temple to monstrosity and human-caused suffering, where slave traders had collected and stored Africans before shipping them away. The building was both Arab and colonial in style, a warren of hallways with small and big doors, each one intricately carved, each one a portal to ruined lives.

I felt trapped. The whole city felt menacing, insidious. Men scowled and leered at women, especially black women, black women hanging around white women most of all. In restaurants locals assumed that I was the translator for my Yale group or that I was their whore.

A worker or a whore—not an American, not a Yalie, not the Oprah Girl, not special, not strong, not brave. "No. I am a student!" I said in Swahili and then Kinyarwanda. "I am a STUDENT!" But after dropping that one piece of my biography, I stopped talking. My frenzied rage pleased the locals. They called me Angry Brown Sugar.

There was one other black girl on our trip, but she was very light-skinned and she wore blond braids. She could blend in. My skin was dark, almost ebony from the equatorial sun.

When locals would talk to us and address only the white people at the table, I wanted to scream, *Those kids don't give a shit. They know nothing about your life. And I'm sitting here. I know exactly who you are, I've lived your life, and I'm the lowest person in this whole situation?*

Mombasa designated a section of beachfront for white tourists and their escorts. This was the most debased kind of travel—fifty-year-old European men with fifteen-year-old Kenyan girls.

On the streets, too, and in the clubs, more old men with

young girls. Maybe they'd seen a Facebook picture of a friend marrying a rich white man and they thought marriage would be their ticket. Maybe they thought they'd fall in love. Older white women walked the streets with handsome young black lovers. It all looked better than Fort Jesus.

Men and money, men and candy. The story never stopped. A man who rode a motorcycle would visit our house, when I still lived with my parents in Kigali. Always he brought candy. My mom told me that's how girls are tricked—men give you things. They lie and they give you things. After that I refused and said to the man, "Oh, I don't like candy."

I hate candy to this day. The second and third time the man visited, he gave me a look of disgust that I would not take his candy. I remember he visited neighbors' houses too, the houses of two girls I played with. Some girls took the candy in a heartbeat.

Maybe this was why I didn't have friends: because I yelled, *He's going to ruin you.*

I REBELLED AND STARTED WEARING spaghetti straps. I wore short skirts. I walked alone. It was dangerous and stupid. I was so scared that the person I'd created would be lost, that she was already lost. My fears multiplied. I was scared that the Yale group would fly home and leave me behind. I was scared that I would be sold. I was scared that I would be killed.

I can see now that I broadcast my fears, dropped them like seeds in fertile soil, and made them come true. As I walked through the city, I got catcalled. I got groped. I got pushed up against a wall. I wanted to prove to myself that I could hold on to who I was through the assault. I wanted to prove I could be like Claire: inviolable. I wanted to prove that I could be rejected, disparaged, and still no one could make me feel small.

The cats in Mombasa screeched and meowed like they were getting beaten. I heard them in my dreams, and in my dreams I responded to their tormentors in Swahili so I'd have rehearsed the language to defend myself when I woke.

When not in class I read in my room, hoping to unearth the secret to hate.

I found an essay in a book called *Illuminations* by Walter Benjamin, in which every time the men go off to war they lose all their language. When they return home they can't describe to their families what they saw, so they go back to war to learn the words again.

I bought $200 worth of beads. I made nothing with them. I had a dream about shoving things into a closet. In the dream, I opened the closet door, intending to cram my *katundu* inside, only to find all the objects already there.

Near the end of our stay we spent a few days on the island of Lamu. Lamu had resisted colonization. It still had no roads, only footpaths for people and donkeys. There, I finally got the reaction I wanted. "You live in America," people said, "and you speak Swahili? Come to our house and sit and drink tea."

But when we returned to mainland Mombasa all my fears and anger returned. The nightmares that I would be lost. The nightmares that I would be stolen. The nightmares that I would be sold.

I returned to Chicago early.

. . .

BACK IN KENILWORTH, AT THE Thomases', I put on my shorts and running shoes and ran along Sheridan Road, relieved to be in a place where I felt safe and did not have to think constantly about my body.

Then, a few days before flying back to New Haven for the start of school, I went to the drugstore to pick up a prescription. I'd been babysitting, so I was wearing leggings and a T-shirt. My hair was a mess. The pharmacist gave me a hard time.

"I'm in the system," I said. "I have insurance." I was still on the Thomases' plan.

The pharmacist was curt. "I'm sorry, ma'am," she said. "I can't find it. You're not in the system." *Next.*

Her tone was absolute, cocky and dismissive. I thought, *Fine. You want to judge my body? Fine.*

I returned to the Thomases', showered, put on makeup, dressed up like a Kenilworth girl, changed my walk to a nice Kenilworth girl walk, my voice to a nice Kenilworth girl voice. I returned to the pharmacy and approached the pharmacist again. She did not recognize me, or admit she recognized me. I got my pills and left.

17

S ay something happens—say a bird hits this window right here. You and I, we're strangers in our strange costumes. We've come to this moment from different places. I might be terrified of the smash and the carnage, recoil as if the bird were a bomb. You might think I'm overreacting and say, *It's just a bird.*

What's wrong with me? Or what's wrong with you? If I don't share with you my history, if I don't explain what I've brought with me to this moment in time—that to me the bird hitting the window sounded like a shell detonating—then how could you know me? If I'm shaking, trying to bring myself back to objective reality, saying to myself, *It's a bird, right? It's a bird, right? It's a bird, right?* and I don't share with you my trauma, I alienate myself. I push you away.

All the things that we do not say create not just space

but a force field between us, a constant, energetic pressure. Two people in pain are magnets, repelling each other. We cannot or will not reach across the space to connect.

So much of Rwanda—so much of the world—struggles with this. When you're traumatized, your sense of self, your individuality, is beaten up. Your skin color, your background, your pain, your hope, your gender, your faith, it's all defiled. Those essential pieces of yourself are stolen. You, as a person, are emptied and flattened, and that violence, that theft, keeps you from embodying a life that feels like your own. To continue to exist, as a whole person, you need to re-create, for yourself, an identity untouched by everything that's been used against you. You need to imagine and build a self out of elements that are not tainted. You need to remake yourself on your own terms.

I understand, now, that to accomplish this, I need more than the artifacts stuffed into a suitcase. I need to comprehend my history, a deep history. I know the facts about the genocide—the intentional savagery of the killings, the use of rape and the spread of HIV as instruments of war. But that is not enough. That past, that story, cannot fill me. I need a longer, broader, more fully human backstory, a history not all soaked in blood. I need clarity, perspective, joy, beauty, originality, intelligence, a wide-angle view.

But the truth is, I already know how to take the next step in life, and it is simple. I need to be brave and vulnerable. I need to reach across space, take my mother's hand, and share my joy and pain.

This is so hard.

. . .

MY SECOND FALL AT YALE I started looking at my hands—they were my mother's hands. I looked at my feet—my right foot in particular, it was one of my father's feet. I kept trying to understand myself through academics as well—psychology, history, and political science—and still I found that approach overly abstract and literal, and hard-hearted.

Then my photography professor asked the class to read a poem about a girl in Connecticut walking to school in the cold. She wanted to take the train, but she was black and blacks weren't allowed.

For the next session of that photography class, the professor took us on a field trip to the Prudence Crandall School for Negro Girls in Canterbury, Connecticut. I did not learn this until later, but an abolitionist named Prudence Crandall opened the school in 1831. At first she enrolled only white girls. Then she admitted one black girl, and a bunch of the white girls withdrew. The school closed for a time. It reopened, in 1833, for black girls only. In 1834 a mob of angry, threatened neighbors attacked the building with iron bars and clubs. After that, the Prudence Crandall School for Negro Girls closed for good.

When we arrived, our professor said, "Sometimes what is not written is the strongest memory we have. It's in the air, so I want you to find it."

She instructed us just to wander the school, take in the space, and put together a story from the details we saw and felt.

This was the first time I was told to set myself in the way of memory and believe in what I experienced.

This was the first time that I was told that the story, all the information I needed, was already there. I just needed to slow down and know how to look, how to listen. I needed to trust that the lingering details contained the whole history.

The Prudence Crandall School for Negro Girls had been meticulously restored, the building stately and closed-lipped, with gables, fluted pilasters, and twin chimneys. We milled around in silence for three hours. I felt the same revulsion that had flooded over me as soon as we landed in Mombasa.

The fear, the claustrophobia, the sense of being hunted. I was back in the school with Claire, the one with no panes in the windows, the playground outside. I felt my hatred well up. I heard the woman crying, her cries that would not cease.

THERE WAS A BOOK CALLED *On the Natural History of Destruction,* by W. G. Sebald. It sounded like my history, so I signed up for a seminar on his work.

The class was taught by a comparative literature professor named Carol Jacobs. She had hooded eyes, exhausted eyes, but they were unwavering. Her thick German accent soothed me. She was both there and not there, engaged and deeply taken by her own thoughts.

Professor Jacobs's first lecture to us was a warning. Be careful with assuming you understand Sebald. Be careful with thinking that you know what he thinks. Be careful with your assumptions about the way he presents space. Be careful with your assumptions about the way he presents time. Be careful with your assumptions about the images too—he will use images from a contemporary museum in New York and place them in Europe in the past. Be careful with your assumptions about the way he presents stories, because some people in his book really exist and others do not. Be careful with your assumptions about the truth. Your assumptions will not be of any service in this class.

Our job, Professor Jacobs said, was to be on all the time, to interrogate the details of our lives and create maps, however incomplete, of our interior worlds.

Sebald is not an easy writer. He's intense and inscrutable, a German born near the end of the Holocaust but not a Jew, a man who came of age in a country that destroyed itself. He dropped into his books random-seeming photographs of libraries, eyes, animals, windows, and trees.

Professor Jacobs told us to expect to be confused, to embrace the confusion. Sebald did not intend to provide enough information. The odd images, the looping thoughts, the disorientation produced by the two—these were meant to capture the mass amnesia that fell over Germany after World War II.

In my Sebald class was a Mexican or Chilean boy—I never figured it out. He spoke with a spectacular sense of authority, tossing about references to semiotic literary theory. I had no idea what he was saying. I found him inspiring.

I can still pick up Sebald's *Austerlitz* and read any sentence and it feels like the whole world. The book was my flashlight, my looking glass, my everything. The novel is about a middle-aged man who, as an infant during World War II, was shipped out of Czechoslovakia by his Jewish parents on the *Kindertransport,* an organized effort to save Jewish children by sending them to be raised in Britain. He spends his entire adult life searching, feeling inchoate, dislocated, lost. Nobody ever tells him about his past.

Sebald tells this story through a gorgeous haze, following Austerlitz as he tries to piece together his life story from his obsessions, curiosities, and habits of mind. Austerlitz's parents died in the war, when he was still a young child. He sees traces of them everywhere.

I was mesmerized immediately. On page 9 Austerlitz describes Belgium as "a little patch of yellowish gray barely visible on the map of the world." Belgium: *a little patch, barely visible*. Belgium, the country that colonized and brutalized Rwanda. Belgium, the country that changed everything, that ruined everything. If I looked at it from the right perspective, in the right light, it was pathetic, yellowish, and small.

Before taking this class, I'd often felt that my feelings were wrong, that my reactions to places were wrong, as my feelings and reactions were not consistent from day to day. Sometimes the architecture at Yale terrified me; other times it made me feel safe. That internal flip-flopping, I assumed, pointed to something flimsy in my thinking or unstable in my mind.

Sebald showed me that we live in all times and places at once. His central preoccupation was a kind of physics, an attempt to define and describe what he called "the laws governing the return of the past." The past is all in there, all the time, a dark cauldron, bubbling. Different triggers cause different thoughts to rise to the surface at different times. All that changes is what we see in the moment.

. . .

EACH DAY I MADE A practice of walking by Annette, a woman who stood in front of the Hall of Graduate Studies with a bucket of flowers that she purchased in bunches at the grocery store and sold as singles for a tiny profit. Almost nobody noticed her.

She had nothing to do with most students' impressive, Ivy League lives. But to me, in my new Sebaldian mindset, she became a link to a buried past, a reminder of Claire selling goat meat, bras, anything, to get us out of our deadening refugee lives.

I'd been a masterful observer for so long, but I'd put that skill to use as a mimic and a chameleon, not as a detective. I gathered details, evidence, gestures and styles, and regurgitated them. I saw my aptitude as a trick, my hustle. Mimicry bought you the keys to the kingdom.

I had never considered using my skills for myself, gathering evidence about myself, scrutinizing my own tells and tics. But Professor Jacobs told us to be on all the time, to investigate all the time, to analyze everything, to believe it all had meaning.

I had tried therapy several times over the years, but it always felt too direct, too invasive, too medicalized. That Rembrandt painting *The Anatomy Lesson of Dr. Nicolaes Tulp,* that's what therapy felt like to me. On the canvas a group of eight men who look nearly identical, all rosy-cheeked and bearded, in black frocks and white collars, stand around gawking at the body of a ninth man who is naked, dead, and ghoulishly white, and whose arm is skinned and flayed. The image is voyeuristic, and to me, distasteful, both for its peering inside the dead, defenseless body, and for the smug, entitled looks on the faces of the men in frocks. They seem to feel all the world is theirs to toy with and probe, even this body in death.

Now here was Sebald, telling me I didn't need to do that. I didn't need to peel off my skin until I screamed, I didn't need to expose my wounds for others. I could work the problem myself. I could take my whole world as my text. I could learn to understand my own mind.

His books offered a method, or at least implied one: if a person wades deep enough into memory and pays close enough attention to the available clues, a narrative will emerge that makes moral and emotional sense.

His theory of memory meant that the residue of my history was already there. I just needed to ask the right questions and look for answers with a discerning eye. Why did I use the GPS map on my phone, even on campus, when I knew where I was going? Why did I talk so much—was I afraid I'd disappear? Why did I drink only tea, never cold water? Why did I cringe when the sun turned red?

After seeing Annette, I turned down Prospect Street and took pictures of the roots and vines growing outside Yale's Grove Street Cemetery. I wanted to find order and connection in the world. I wanted a live link, a route back, to all of my dead who were not buried and never would be. I studied the patterns in the images of the cemetery vines to see if they matched the patterns of the veins in my hands.

THE FOLLOWING SUMMER I INTERNED at Google, in the diversity program. One day our program director instructed all of us to show up early and surprised us by saying, "We're going to Disneyland!" A van drove us to the San Francisco airport.

On the short flight to Los Angeles I told a coworker about my Mickey Mouse backpack. It still made me cry.

His response was perfect. "Clem," he said, "we're going to do EVERYTHING."

Disneyland stunned me: not just the employees walking around in Minnie and Mickey suits, a surreal, joyful reminder of my lost treasure. The whole place was, to me, a paradise, a triumph of imagination, a testament to the possibility of assembling a self and saying to yourself, *What do you think happened next?* and then making that story come true. I bought cotton candy and ate it without fear. I floated through It's a Small World. I was in Walt Disney's world, inside his imagination and no one else's. My favorite ride was Pirates of the Caribbean—I loved being on that boat. It wasn't the boat of all my nightmares. It was just *ibulayi,* away.

18

I had long assumed the ghosts of my past would keep me from ever wanting to return to Rwanda. I had barely recovered from Kenya. Yet during my sophomore year at Yale, when I was twenty-two, a woman on campus asked me to join her spring-break trip to Rwanda. She was part of a group that had fund-raised to buy water tanks for the Agahozo-Shalom Youth Village, a community in Rwanda funded by Americans and modeled on a kibbutz in Israel set up for Holocaust orphans. This Yale group was flying over in March to install the water tanks. I agreed to go.

On the plane, Zach told me everything would be fine. He was in far over his head. I panicked throughout the flight and we arrived at the youth village late at night. I took an Ambien but still woke before sunrise. Before I left I'd promised myself that while in Rwanda I would just sit with my pain. I would not bury it, display it, or disavow it. I would keep it as my own.

The sunrise was bright orange—the orange of disaster, the orange of safety cones, the orange that Pudi had once told me meant that a nun or priest had died. Zach took a picture of me sitting on the porch, half awake, regarding the dawn. My hair is wild and unbraided, and I look relieved.

THAT FEELING DIDN'T LAST. I studied more Sebald. I made more dresses to try to purge my demons. I introduced Elie Wiesel at the Holocaust Memorial Museum in Washington, DC, and President Obama appointed me to the board. It was such an honor, and a great solace, to work with those committed to remembering. Then, in 2014, when I was twenty-six, I flew to Kigali with a delegation from the museum for an event to commemorate the twentieth anniversary of the Rwandan genocide.

I was the youngest person in the group, the chosen emissary to tell the story of genocide to future generations. I was also the only Rwandan. From the airport, a van took our delegation to our hotel. I told myself I was fine, though I still scanned every room for exits, in case I needed to run, and I still meticulously read people's faces and body language so I would know exactly how they wanted me to walk and talk, what they wanted me to do.

The air in Kigali smelled like orange and lemon blossoms. The streets were clean, no one begged. The city, nestled among the hills, looked like a provincial capital in Tuscany, modern yet still pastoral, churches galore, a few bigger office buildings downtown, cell phone purveyors on every corner. Not far from the Kigali Genocide Memorial, a gorgeous new public library had opened—glass walls, soaring ceilings, all light, intelligence, hope, and space. The whole country felt to me like it was engaged in that project: holding its chin high, determined not to swivel around to see who might be creeping up from behind. The burden of history, the presence of history, was overwhelming. Rwanda did its best to contain and partition off the past by labeling everything prior to the genocide *before*. The word "before" is simple yet effective: that was then, this is now; so clean, so Zen (before genocide chop wood, carry water; after genocide chop wood, carry water), a look out to the horizon over a windless ocean, so smooth, so blue, no corpses floating on the surface, no body parts sticking out.

Now, at nearly every major intersection stood young men with guns, pants tucked into their shiny black boots. They watched the traffic and the passersby. I hated this and yet Rwanda needed this. We had brought this on ourselves. When a country's citizens start killing one another, you need to reestablish order, you make a display of safekeeping. You can't allow everybody to sink into their totally reasonable fears.

That first night we all ate dinner at Hôtel des Mille Collines, the "Hotel Rwanda" of the film to my traveling companions, though to me it was the hotel where my mother's brother used to take us swimming. He'd buy us ice cream and we'd sit under the umbrellas in the shade. When we left he always joked, "I better keep working hard so I can keep buying you ice cream!"

He was now dead. Not called to God—dead.

. . .

ON OUR SECOND DAY THERE, I dressed up and, along with the other women in the Holocaust Memorial Museum delegation, went to a luncheon with the First Lady at the President's house. All the streets in Kigali were numbered now—they hadn't been named or numbered before. Most of the trees had been cut down. Everything out of the shadows, into the light. Nowhere to hide.

The tablecloth was embroidered with chain-stitched flowers and birds. The First Lady was elegant and gracious. She wanted to hear our stories and she wanted to tell us hers.

The Rwandan government now had an official narrative. Before the Belgians arrived and colonized Rwanda, Hutus and Tutsis lived in peace. But colonization is built on the idea that we are not the same, that we don't possess equal humanity. The Belgians imposed their cruel ideology: their belief that people with certain-sized skulls and certain-width noses were better and smarter than others, that they belonged to a superior race.

This ideology leached into the Rwandan psyche and caused the country to self-destruct.

ON THE MORNING OF REMEMBRANCE DAY, a bus came to the hotel to drive us to Amahoro Stadium. I had a hard time believing this event was happening in a stadium at all. Twenty years earlier, in eastern Rwanda, government officials had told people to gather in Gatwaro Stadium. Twelve thousand did. They were all murdered.

Still, we rode toward the horror. People arrived at the stadium from all parts of Rwanda, switching from one bus to another, walking for days, because this was the anniversary, the one time of the year Rwandans were permitted to grieve. Before the government had designated a grieving season—a period of one hundred days beginning on April 7—the country had existed in unstoppable tumult and upheaval, its citizens constantly wailing, screaming obscenities, burning things in anger.

With the exception of that hundred days, Rwandans greeted one another with the word *komera*. Everyone was gentle, firm, wary, and opaque. *Komera* means "be strong."

A marching band played as we entered the stadium. I sat in the VIP section with the others from the Holocaust museum. On my seat was a small gift box with a beaded Remembrance Day pin. None of the Rwandans behind me knew who I was or that I was one of them. I wanted to disappear. I had brought a scarf and now I closed myself inside it. I kept on my sunglasses. I did not want to see.

All around me, people started screaming. First one woman, then another, then another. Then the men. The Remembrance Day program began with an extremely compressed reenactment of the history of Rwanda, from colonialism to the present day—singing, dancing, a huge production. More than six hundred people performed. Everybody knew the basic plot.

"Dehumanization started. And humans became objects," a voice blared over the public address system. A few minutes later the dancers who played the white colonizers morphed into the white aid workers.

Several minutes after that, hundreds of Rwandan actors pantomimed killing and death.

The screaming continued throughout. Unhinged. The wailing became so florid, so vibrant, so volcanic and out of control that guards in yellow vests began carrying out the most spastic of the bereaved. On the stadium floor the actors playing peacekeeping soldiers from the current government brought the dead Rwandans back to life.

I didn't like the staging, but what staging would have been right? There was no way to do this—to gather the country for a few hours to remember nearly a million lives exterminated and the millions more destroyed.

President Kagame, lithe, sophisticated, and somber, stood up to speak. He explained to the assembled, and to the world, that Rwandans needed to unite and heal themselves, because if we didn't take care of ourselves, nobody would.

Kagame, during his speech, switched from English to Kinyarwanda and back again, so that both the dignitaries and his citizens would understand. The genocide was the fault of colonization, he said, a grotesque reflection of a diseased mentality, the Europeans' dark id. The narrative strategy Kagame deployed in his speech made sense. He offered a simple, digestible story: *The Belgians came, spread evil, and left. The rest of us remained here.*

We needed to find a way to tolerate an intolerable truth. We needed to acknowledge facts that are incompatible with a stable faith in humanity, incompatible even with any sane definition of God.

The speeches continued. The crying continued. The

screaming continued throughout. The guards in yellow vests removed two hundred–some people from the stadium. There was so much pain. I felt profoundly ashamed. I did not want to be an emissary of this. I did not want to keep telling this story to future generations. It would destroy me. I wanted instead to crawl inside my scarf. I wanted to be blown away.

A woman next to me fainted. I found myself wondering whether she was real or if I hallucinated her. She could not be real, yet her body was right there.

I flew home and stayed in bed for a week.

A YEAR LATER I TRAVELED to Israel with the Carter Center as part of a delegation to learn about refugees. I packed my books and my candles and I visited the Aida Refugee Camp, just a mile from Bethlehem, in the West Bank. The refugees here were Palestinian. This was the first time I'd been in a camp where the residents didn't look like me.

Near the end of the trip we visited the security fence, the giant barrier of concrete and concertina wire that separates Israel and Palestine. I'd read about it, I knew about the walls, but seeing this monstrosity, this monument to intimidation and fear, and then lining up to pass through security . . . it shut me down. You see men with guns. You see children with guns. You're herded by disembodied voices into a space that feels like a cattle chute.

From there you turn a corner and the walls are green, blank planes of gray and green, and there are just voices, disembodied voices, issuing commands. The voices, the commands, they make you feel small. You don't see a man.

You don't see a person. You are not a person. You are just hearing a voice.

My shoes caused trouble. I was wearing black boots, almost like soldier boots, leather with a two-inch heel and a silver buckle on the side. I had worn the boots in Rwanda.

The guards at the gate wanted to know about my boots. The security agents at the airport did too. Those agents interrogated me for two hours. I cried much of the time. They wanted to know where I'd bought my boots. Where I wore them. What I was doing in Israel. What I was doing in Palestine. They made me take them off and they scanned them.

I was interested in why they cared—Sebald gave me that. What did my boots mean for them? What could the moment teach me?

After I got my boots back, I composed myself and ran to the gate. The guards stopped me again. They pulled me aside and dug through my carry-on bags. I was on my period. I had loose tampons and extra underwear in there. They pulled them out, regarded them. I felt humiliated.

By the time I boarded the plane I was crying, again. I cried all the time. I was flying first class, but no level of service or amount of champagne could shut down that whole nightmare.

Still, I had my American passport. I could get out of there.

19

The elementary school girls at the Palm Beach Day Academy all wore matching yellow jumpers. The boys wore white cotton polo shirts, each embroidered with PBDA in navy thread. I'd flown down to Palm Beach from New Haven to speak, and as always, for my talk, I dressed up: A-line dress, high heels. I did not look approachable; I looked commanding. And yet the students, all soft-cheeked and porous, looked at me with their full-moon eyes, so guileless and sweet.

After the assembly wrapped up and we all left the auditorium, I noticed, in the corridor, one little girl staring at me, unabashed. She began to walk toward me, then got shy and ducked behind her teacher, who, in turn, crouched beside the child and whispered with such gentleness, "You can go say hi."

It was nothing, yet it shook something loose in me. I'd

forgotten how tender adults could be with other people's children. That girl felt safe, here in this lovely school, with no more protection than her teacher's leg.

I have never been a gentle protectress. I love Claire's kids, but I have actively, deliberately destroyed their tenderness. My way of caretaking was militarized. My job was to shield them from harm and death. I prepared them for the worst.

Those kids didn't have a safety margin, no cushion, not even adequate supervision. Claire's children and my younger siblings, plus a young cousin who also lived with Claire, they watched TV until 11:00 p.m. and fell asleep in class. They were the last kids picked up each day at their schools' aftercare programs, due to Claire's schedule, and if Claire's boss kept her overtime, or if the train was slow, she was even later.

One Friday afternoon I came home and found Freddy and his friends sprawled on the couches after football practice, watching sports. I exploded. "Do you know someone else is taking practice SSAT tests right now? Why is your room not clean? Why are the dishes not washed?"

Freddy said, "It's Friday."

"I know it's the weekend! I don't care that it's the weekend! Tell those kids to get out of the house." I yelled at Freddy's friends too. "Go home and read something. Don't watch these stupid shows." They all hated me.

We were all so broken. I was so broken. I should have been lashing out at the world, but I was yelling at these specific children. I was not safe. I was not gentle.

When I returned from Palm Beach Day Academy, I had a new mission: to get Claire's kids away from us, at least part of the time. I was adept at working the system; I knew where to find scholarships, how to fill out the financial aid forms. I knew that if a school's admissions committee had doubts about one of our kids' academic preparedness, we could offer to repeat a grade.

So I set Claire's children on the path I had followed: Mariette left to do a post-graduate semester at the African Leadership Academy in South Africa, then went to American University in Washington, DC; Freddy attended Mooseheart Child City & School near Chicago, and then enrolled at Milton Academy, a boarding school outside Boston; Michele followed Freddy to Milton three years later. When he was a freshman, Freddy was a star of the football team, roundly adored, and on the cover of the school magazine. We were good Americans, when we wanted to be.

I HAD NO HOME OF my own after I graduated from college. I could not return to the Thomases'. They had given me everything that they had given to their own children. Mrs. Thomas understood me at my most vulnerable and looked out for me. She knew if she moved the things in my room while I was away I'd have to rearrange them. She always had popcorn and chamomile tea. But I felt I had to move on, grow up. I could not live, again, in Kenilworth. I could not go back to Claire's. I could not go live with my parents and define myself again as their child. Not even my younger siblings lived with my parents—they lived with Claire.

I did have options—gorgeous, generous options. I could fly to New York and stay for a month in a friend's fancy apartment. I could fly to Palm Beach, be a guest at another lovely, glamorous home, and attend Gatsby-style parties and laugh with blond, tanned girls.

But then what? More travel? More luxury? More filling and refilling and sampling and imbibing, more saying "yes, please" and "thank you very much," a cycle I now knew would never end because I still hadn't filled, hadn't even fully acknowledged, the vast emptiness inside me.

This became a kind of madness, a repetition dysfunction, a way to keep the story in motion, keep smiling the beads, but never settle on a denouement. I needed to pause. I needed stability. My boyfriend, Ryan, an East Coast hockey player I started dating at Yale after Zach and I split up, wanted to move to California. He was gentle, patient, and good to me. He also had no interest in Sebald, no compulsion to interrogate the details of his life. This annoyed me at times, but mostly it made me feel safe and in control. So I moved, we moved.

I rented a place near Lafayette Park, in one of San Francisco's few classic old apartment buildings. I did yoga, sometimes twice a day. I walked in the Berkeley Hills. Those hills looked like Rwanda.

IN PUBLIC, I PLAYED THE part of myself. I wore the right makeup, the right jewelry, the right dress. I was nobody and I was everybody. But no role felt exactly right. Each performance felt distancing, a ruse.

I stood in front of audiences and tried to package my story in a way that mattered. Sometimes people listened, sometimes they didn't listen. Some people seemed amazed and moved, and some looked bored and proud of themselves, like they were checking a box.

"Here's my story," I said. "Use it now or later. When you need it, it'll be there for you. Maybe someday you'll be facing a challenge, and you'll think of my story. You'll think of Claire. You'll remember to put your ego in a bag and throw that bag away. You'll remember to be kind and generous and a better human. Maybe you'll realize that you need to learn to tell your own. You'll start thinking: *How did I come to have my possessions? How did I come to believe in my God?*

"I know it is a privilege to have the safety, time, comfort, and education to try to shape my experience into something coherent, to think critically and creatively about my life. There's a difference between story and experience. Experience is the whole mess, all that actually happened; a story is the pieces you string together, what you make of it, a guide to your own existence. Experience is the scars on my legs. My story is that they're proof that I'm alive. Your story, the meaning you choose to take when you listen to me, might be different. Your story might be that my scars are my fault and I should feel shame."

Onstage, I tried to be relevant and not too frightening. If I was speaking to my peers, I'd say, "I totally freaked out watching *The Hunger Games*. Maybe you did too? District Nine looked like Zaire during the war." It was true: the feral cats in the ruined buildings, the world drenched in blood and sooty gray.

Almost always I wore my five-inch heels. No doubt people wondered, *Why is a humanitarian speaker wearing those shoes?* But I needed to be stared at, to be admired and loved. I needed to confound people's expectations. I needed to be my own creation: specific, alarming, unique.

The transaction that resulted from sharing my story often bothered me. Some wanted to help me, and could not stand the idea that I was not defeated. Panic flashed across their faces when I suggested to those who considered themselves more powerful than me that the transaction could go both ways. That I could help them too.

I was often cast as a martyr or a saint. I was special, very special. So strong, so brave, a genocide princess, definitely not just one of the many dozens of dark migrant bodies crammed into a flimsy boat, the ones they saw in those horrifying images on the front page of the *New York Times*. But I was still a character out of their imagination, a prisoner of their assumptions. I was not their equal. On occasion I was asked if I felt guilty for surviving.

"Uh, no," I answered. "I did everything I could to survive. Do you think I should feel guilty for surviving? Do you feel guilty that on 9/11 you weren't in one of the Twin Towers?"

ONE WINTER EVENING, A YEAR or so into my San Francisco tenure, I sat on a panel for an international nonprofit that wanted to partner with thought leaders to innovate, or something like that. I was often invited to mingle with haute Silicon Valley. I was a woman—*check*. Black—*check*. A refugee—*check-plus*.

This nonprofit thought they wanted to hear my story and I thought I wanted to tell them. They had declared it

Refugee Week. I would be the representative refugee conversing with the great minds of the new economy about what we should do to help solve the refugee crisis.

The world cared deeply about refugees, for that thirty seconds. Aleppo was under siege. Migrants kept dying in the Mediterranean. Everybody's Instagram and Facebook feeds were lit up with that searing photograph of the drowned baby boy on a beach. The photo was so powerful that whenever I heard the word "refugee" I saw that baby. I saw baby, beach, water, boat, bright blue.

Punctuating this filtered, curated horror was the occasional hero YouTubing from the rubble in Syria. Some of these YouTubing men were born social media stars—so handsome, so articulate, so courageous, so special. This look-how-compassionate-I-am social media extravaganza was certainly better than disregard.

But it was hard to keep all of the many individual lives in focus. Tens of thousands were dying way over there, and look, here is this one precious baby or this one outstanding adult. I understood this. I did it myself. It's truly impossible to hold all the single experiences of suffering in the world in your mind at the same time. The human brain can't handle that much pain. You cannot differentiate and empathize with each of those distinct people. You cannot hear each of their stories and recognize every individual as strong and special, and continue on with your day.

ON THE PANEL WE DISCUSSED the Red Cross and how they should intervene. Then one of my co-panelists mentioned something that he found funny: refugees had started telling aid workers that, in addition to food, water, and shelter, they wanted a way to store photos.

To him this was a laugh line, a classic comedy setup: here we're talking about this big, terrible weighty issue and oh, can we pivot for just a second to this petty first-world concern?

Only it wasn't a laugh line to those involved. I had only those two pictures total of myself in Rwanda. I had only a few photographs of anybody at all in my family from before 2000. This was a never-ending wellspring of confusion. I wanted to see the people I came from. I wanted pictures of those people to help me figure out the person I was and the person I might have been.

But digital storage was not what my co-panelists wanted to discuss. They came here to rescue. They planned on being saviors.

I breathed in and out. I kept my poise. I was extremely good at sitting before a group and keeping my poise. Then, midway through the evening, another one of my co-panelists, a big mensch-y billionaire, turned to me and asked: "So how does it feel to be one of us?"

I recoiled. I had worn purple lipstick that night, just on the inside of my lips. People found that very interesting. "One of us"—what did that mean? One of the rich people? One of the white people? One of the people who'd never been kicked out of the kingdom? One of the people on the top of humanity's heap? One of the people who gives, not takes? One of the people who never suffered? I did not know what he meant by "us" and I did not want to live in his story.

"Actually, I'd rather you ask me how I got to sit here,"

I said, still poised, still smiling, but no longer playing my expected role. "Ask me about my journey," I said. "Ask me why I'm sitting here—what do I know that other refugees don't know, that people suffering from homelessness don't know. What do I know that you don't know. I hacked into your system."

"Let's talk about that after," the billionaire said, uncomfortable that I'd diverged from the check-plus former refugee script. The moderator moved us along.

After the panel, I found the billionaire and asked him if he would like to meet for tea so that we could have that talk. He said to email him to set up a date. I had his email address from the panel organizers.

I wrote but he didn't respond.

20

I was still a hard person to love. I wanted to be adored and admired but not needed. I wanted to retain the right to disappear. Remaining in place, nesting—it set off fears that somebody would yank me away. To counter it, I had to flee. I had to reassure myself that I still knew how to escape.

My body itself remained alien, a burden. I'd had to carry this thing around with me—this body, with its dark skin, unruly hair, and narrow feet; this body, with its liabilities, this body that had been vandalized, stolen. This was the hardest thing in the world: to remember the ravagement and still believe my body was magic, to remember the shattering and still believe my body was spectacular, holy, and capable of creation.

There are moments for which I still have no vocabulary. My mind bounces from the terror and havoc into colors. I say, *It was blue. It was green.* The memory makes me want to burn everything, raze the whole galaxy, and my brain won't hold the plot. But I have to keep trying—we have to keep trying. I have to find a way to tell you: *This happened. Men came, seeking to destroy my body and demolish my future. But I cannot be ruined.*

Rape is the story of women and war, girls and war, hundreds of thousands of mothers, daughters, sisters, grandmothers, cousins, and aunts in my country alone, hundreds of millions across the world. So many men were murdered in the massacre. So many women later died of HIV. Rape, ruin—corporeal, psychological, social—lingered in even the most polished, sophisticated, private spaces decades after the war. *Night* is not a woman's story. Rwandans believe we're comfortable with silence. But silence accommodates hate.

I try to put myself back together, so that I don't fear men or need them to protect me, so I can reclaim my power. These days I read Audre Lorde. She is my light. "We have been taught that silence would save us, but it won't." "I feel, therefore I can be free." "The erotic is a measure between the beginnings of our sense of self and the chaos of our strongest feelings." Any man I invite into my heart and my life needs to understand the magnitude of emotion inside a woman who has gone through war.

When Ryan first told me that he loved me, I was harsh. I said, "Excuse me, what does that even mean? *I. Love. YOU.* Really, what does that mean?" I thought, at the time, that he was imposing his will. I thought, at the time, that his remark was selfish. "Well, if that's the story that you're going to tell yourself, that you love me, I guess you love me," I said.

. . .

RYAN WAS SO PATIENT, so kind, so white and jocky, so detached from my whole African genocide-survivor-girl drama, which was probably the point. His mother had programmed him to be a good Catholic. He played roller hockey. He drove for Uber and Lyft. He sat on the couch in our shared apartment all day on Sunday and watched football or basketball or baseball or movies. He ate chips. I was constantly taking notes.

We spent five years together, Ryan and I. He protected me, adored me, tolerated me. I had lots of rules. He could not call me *cupcake, sugar,* or any food name. He could not describe me as *bossy, sassy, bitchy,* or anything negative.

I needed him, I truly did. Friends asked me to join them at Burning Man. I went, Ryan stayed home. Immediately I realized I'd set myself up. This is where people went to experience ecstasy but also to get closer to suffering—elective, luxury suffering. The desert was hot and dusty, filled with tents. The first morning I woke up and said, *What have I done? Where's the food?* I felt cold. I'd left my blue blanket at home.

That day and night, I wore costumes. I drank, danced, looked at art, and I became disoriented. Time and space became kaleidoscopic, colors spinning, no fixed base. I wanted to return to my tent, so I pulled out my bewildering map. The camp was laid out like a clock. Nothing made sense. The journey back to the tent took hours, days, maybe years. I finally did make it to our camp, and the next morning I woke up and said to myself, *Okay, another day to survive.*

My friends had already left for their day's adventures.

I was all alone. I started to cry, and I picked up my phone and stared at pictures of Claire's kids. *I have a family,* I said to myself. *I am okay. I have a life somewhere beyond here.*

I pulled on clothes and walked outside, and the wind and the heat smacked me like an open palm to the face. I felt dehydrated and confused. I saw a woman I recognized from the day before. She was doing yoga. She looked very happy and relaxed. I was too nervous to approach her and say *I need help,* so I stared at the kids on my phone again and then started crying. "I don't want to be here anymore," I said to nobody in particular but close enough to the woman so that she could hear. "I want to be home."

The woman paused her yoga and walked over and hugged me. She said, "Honey, honey, you're home. You're fine."

RWANDA IS SO BEAUTIFUL, BUT it is filled with too many people who believe they deserve only pain. I want to find another way. On my most recent trip there, I stayed with Uncle, a man who is not really my uncle but who in many ways is my truest family. He lives in Kigali, in a lovely home, with a stately front porch on which he likes to take his breakfast of fruit and sweet tea. His neighborhood is filled with well-kept gardens and smooth paved streets that look like the Berkeley Hills.

Above his dining table is a large framed wedding photograph: Uncle, handsome in his military uniform, holding the arm of his elegant third wife, who just passed away. That photograph is so sad and its presence gives me peace.

I hardly left Uncle's house the five days I was in Kigali.

When I did I mostly went to the Shokola Storytellers Café, on the top floor of the public library. The space was deep inside my comfort zone: furnished with dark wood floors, jute rugs, and clean-lined modern chairs and couches. You could sit on the roof deck, look over the green hills, eat little elegant *mandazi,* and drink single-origin coffee topped with latte art. But driving through the city upset me, all the buildings from *before,* all the new construction. Near Uncle's house, on the hillside overlooking the farmland in Kigali's central valley, was a huge new development, hundreds of new apartments, the architecture self-hating, charmless, and cold. The buildings were sterile white. The plan was for them to stay that way.

The design screamed out: *You who live here do not deserve beauty. We who designed this are stunted, locked in, and ashamed.*

One afternoon, while I was doing laundry, I lay on a blanket in Uncle's garden while my clothes dried on a line. The sun felt rejuvenating. Some ants worked on a ledge in the shade, dismantling a fallen mango. Nearby was a yellow spider. I felt, at last, after all the hundreds of yoga classes I'd taken, like I'd finally exhaled. I was wearing a floral top, black with huge yellow and green flowers, and a bright yellow skirt. I stood out and I fit in, and I felt taken care of in a way that I felt taken care of nowhere else in the world. It had been so long since I felt like that—like a child, like someone else's ward.

Throughout Rwanda now, the last Saturday morning of the month is reserved for *Umuganda.* This is an official government program to get Rwandans to clean up and take care of their country, the physical space, yes, and the scars of the past. Everybody is to come out of their houses and join with their neighbors to tend to their communities—to clean the streets, paint the schools, whatever is necessary.

It's a beautiful idea, a gorgeous device of repair. And still the wounds are there and the history oozes. Everybody did and saw horrible things. No one can remove that from their eyes. The preachers say Lot's wife was turned into a pillar of salt for looking back on her wrecked city. The message in Rwanda, too, is: *Forget, move on*. But still the burnt ruins exist right there, smoldering.

On my most recent visit, the *Umuganda* project in Uncle's neighborhood was to clear an overgrown field. People showed up in sneakers and windbreakers, smiling. They picked up and swung machetes, the tool all Rwandan families keep in their garages for gardening projects like this. Uncle didn't blink. His neighbors didn't blink. They'd grown accustomed to seeing machetes again. I had a hard time with *Umuganda* that morning. I could not bear the ghosts.

Later that day, a man named Vicki, who had lived in our neighborhood and been a friend of Claire's nearly two dozen years before, picked me up in his Toyota at Uncle's house. I said, "Let's go to the new Marriott."

He shook off the idea. "Oh no, that's not a place where I go," he said. "That place is only for rich people. I can't go there."

I knew the story in his mind. He didn't have the right shoes. He wouldn't fit in. He should stay in his lane. He didn't deserve nice things. "Well, today we're going to be rich!" I said. "Let's go." He drove.

We walked in. I ordered us tea. We logged into the wifi and hung out.

As we left I asked Vicki, "How did that feel?"

He said, "It felt so good."

The night before I left Rwanda, Vicki picked me up again and drove me up a steep hillside. We stood on the side of the road, overlooking Kigali. The sun set, and it was beautiful—I knew this intellectually even if I couldn't enjoy that beauty in my heart. The hills turned from green to blue to black, stacks and stacks of hills, a chain going on forever. Vicki pointed across the lowlands to a patch of blinking lights. He said, "That's where we used to live." I raised my phone and took pictures.

Back in his car, on our way home to Uncle's house, Vicki steered us as close to our old neighborhood as he thought I could handle, down the busy street with men selling phone cards, the kids rolling bike tires with sticks, and the Muslim women wearing kitenges as head scarfs, the whole exuberant multicultural mashup of the world I'd lived in before the universe fell apart. Vicki idled the car in front of a corner shop with no sign, ran in, and returned with a brown paper bag of warm chapati, the oil just starting to seep through.

We ate and drove to the church where my parents got married. The chapati was so delicious, a sunrise, a warm bath in my mother's backyard garden, then being wrapped in Claire's perfect hand-me-down robe. The church looked the same.

A FEW MONTHS BEFORE THAT TRIP, on my twenty-ninth birthday, Ryan and I went for a walk in the Berkeley Hills, on a trail that runs through my favorite park. We started to talk about getting married, but I could not live in that fairy tale.

That story line, to me, was about possession—*to have and to hold, until death do us part.*

Humans are not meant to be possessed.

Ryan also loved me more than I loved myself, and I could not tolerate that. I pushed him away. I needed to learn to hold my own pain. I needed to figure out how to embrace my darkest corners, and when I returned from my trip to Rwanda, he was gone. We'd been coming unglued. My excavation of the past and my constant travel were not easy to live with, and now he'd taken everything. I had told him, many times, that being left was one of my deepest fears. I had always been so scared that Claire would leave me, that one day she'd just get up and hustle off if I wasn't good enough or fast enough, if I didn't follow the rules.

The first thing I noticed, when I entered the apartment and set down my big black suitcase, was that Ryan's guitar was gone. He kept it propped on a stand in the living room by the TV. The guitar wasn't there, the stand wasn't there. I walked into our bedroom. I noticed his phone charger— good. Ryan needed his phone charger. He could not have left. But the door to our closet was wide open. Ryan's shirts were all missing.

All my fears rushed into the room. Shit, shit, shit, the stealing, the faces, the water, the bodies. It all rushed in.

I stood in my bedroom and tried to breathe. I reminded myself: *I live here. I'm home.*

21

I was constantly yearning for mothers, cultivating backup and replacement mothers. I'd never really given mine a shot. Even as an educated, worldly adult, I didn't know how to make the relationship work.

So I invited my mother on a trip with me to Europe. I would restage our reunion. Last time the set and the surprise plot twist were all wrong, out of our control. No one had asked me, *And what do you think happened next?* This time I would do it better.

My mother and I hadn't spent time alone together in twenty years. I flew to London ahead of her. I wanted everything to be perfect—every detail thoughtful and wondrous, like the egg filled with glitter that I'd received as an invitation from a secret society in college. The shell had been hollowed out and refilled with gold sparkles, and in the center was a tiny note. I wanted to give my mother a gift like that. I wanted to invite her to that reunion.

Before my mother arrived, I walked to the West Brompton grocery store and bought fruit, bread, milk, tea, eggs, rice, and a chicken. I bought a bouquet of wild roses and arranged them in a vase next to her bed. On the coverlet I laid out the white nightgown and robe I'd brought along for her as gifts, and in the closet I hung the new wardrobe items I'd purchased for her: two new blouses, two new dresses, a few scarves and skirts.

I wanted my mother to feel special. I wanted her to know her worth. I wanted people to smile at her with great approval whenever she walked into a room.

I TOOK THE TRAIN BACK to Gatwick to meet my mother's plane. I waited and waited in the entrance hall. My mother didn't show. Finally I called her. She was lost. She didn't know the way, so she'd just sat down.

I asked her to pass her phone to a nearby stranger, any stranger, so I could ask this person to please show my mother out. I felt so guilty, so irresponsible. I had not given my mother the address of the West Brompton house. She had never traveled on her American passport and never alone.

At last she emerged, the final person to exit customs from her flight. She was wearing new jeans and carrying a sparkly new bag. Her hair was tightly braided and her nails freshly painted. "I'm so sorry, I'm so sorry," she said, over and over. I called us an Uber. A fancy black car arrived.

"Goodness! Clemantine!" my mother said. On the drive into the city she held her face in her hands, tugged her thumbs, and fell asleep.

She loved the nightgown. She loved the robe. She loved the flowers. She loved the clothes. I rubbed the essential oils I'd packed on my mother's feet. She settled into a nap. When she woke and walked downstairs, a white housekeeper was in the kitchen. The owners of the flat had sent the housekeeper to check on us.

"Does that woman live here?" my mother asked when she left.

I said no and pointed to a picture of the black family who did.

My mother looked so confused.

I HAD MAPPED EVERYTHING OUT—how long each bus ride would take, where we'd get on and off. I took my mother to Westminster Abbey. I found the life-size effigies creepy but my mother loved them. The dead had been chiseled with such serene faces. Some had their hands over their hearts, others had hands pressed in prayer. They were with God.

I planned to show my mother the Infirmarer's Garden. I'd learned online that it once had been planted with roses, lilies, beans, onions, and fruit trees. Now the garden had only green grass that nobody was allowed to step on. A sign said it was closed.

I approached a guard and told him our story: I'd planned this whole trip with such care, my mother and I hadn't spent time alone together in twenty years. The point of my story was: *This moment is important, essential even.* I was telling him and myself: *This moment is essential. It will glue us back together. It will glue me back together.* I still felt broken inside.

The guard let us in. There was something eerie about all this spiky grass on which no one ever walked. My mother started touching all the cobblestones. She wanted to feel and grab everything, every paver, rock. I did not want to be alone with her.

The next day we toured more cathedrals. We visited shops, we tried on clothes. Back in the apartment, for dinner, I roasted the chicken I'd put in the refrigerator and my mother did the dishes. I told her she could leave them for the housekeeper, that the housekeeper would be paid to do them, but my mother insisted. She washed the dishes so slowly that I could not stand to watch. She did not know how luxurious and indulgent it looked to me to wash dishes at that pace. My life did not involve doing chores calmly, as if there was peace.

I felt so overwhelmed to be with just my mother in this apartment, to try to create a whole world from the meager shreds at hand. I wanted my mother to know all the places I'd been, all the horrible things I'd seen, all the scrubbing I'd done in miserable camps, the unthinkable variety of suffering I'd witnessed just to fight my way here, to be in this apartment, to bring her that new white nightgown and white bathrobe. But I didn't want to tell her about my experience. Neither Claire nor I had ever told her our story. I'd never shared even the cleaned-up version I told in public. I'd never felt I could. I still could not now. I felt so furious at myself. I kept shouting in my mind: *Mom, you have no idea.*

. . .

WE TOOK A TRAIN TO PARIS. I found the best croissants. I found the perfect strawberries, the small ones with the green stems attached. I took my mother to quaint boutiques. She stood in front of a three-way mirror and admired a green brocade coat. Then, just as she started admiring herself in it, she gasped at the price and nervously returned the coat to the rack. I bought it for her anyway. I wanted her to believe that she deserved the best coat in the world.

Later that day we attended a lovely lunch at a friend's house. My mother was pampered and catered to—"Would you like fish? Would you like lamb? Would you like that lamb cooked medium rare? Oh, what a lovely coat you have!"

I was trying so hard. The itinerary I'd created was working according to plan, but I had not planned for these feelings. I felt profoundly alone. My mind and my heart seemed disconnected, both underwater, all the communication signals between them distorted and dampened.

My mother and I walked through the Tuileries Garden. She wrinkled her brow, unimpressed by the lazy French planting and pruning. I tried, for a moment, to close the gap between the present and the past, to come out from under the water and speak to her in the clear air.

"Do you miss your own garden?" I asked. A softball, I thought, the easiest possible question to ask about our past lives together, about before.

The life drained from my mother's face. She did not answer.

. . .

WE CONTINUED ON, TO THE LOUVRE. My mother's favorite images, like her favorite stories, were from the Bible. She had a picture of white Jesus on her phone case—ivory skin, blue irises, smooth hair. I wished my mother would see beyond this simple, innocent face. I wished she could see how people had wielded that face to brainwash others, to destroy cultures, to eliminate entire languages, to cause so much degradation and pain. Earlier that day we'd walked by the most gorgeous Senegalese and Nigerian men selling little Eiffel Tower pens and key chains by a metro station. In their eyes you could see they'd suffered as much as my mother's Jesus. Why not pray to them?

The crowds in the museum carried us toward the gallery with the *Mona Lisa*. The space was so packed with humanity. I tried to find the edge of the swarm but failed. I'd hated crowds since our first walk, behind the Red Cross trucks, to our first refugee camp. At a huge painting called *The Wedding Feast at Cana,* I said, "Mom, stop."

The Wedding Feast at Cana depicts a feast, a meal for royalty, and around the table sit Jesus, the apostles, kings, queens, and emperors. They are all alabaster, apparently pure. Everyone whose skin is even a little bit shaded, or who is not well dressed, is either serving those eating or is under the table.

I asked my mother what she saw in the painting.

"That's Jesus right in the middle," she said. "That's Jesus and Mary and the apostles at a feast—a wedding feast."

"What else?" I asked, now slightly caustic. "What does it look like to you?"

"It looks like heaven," she said.

"But, Mom, what is that about, that idea of heaven? Who is it for? See that boy? See that little black boy?" I pointed to the bottom of the painting. "He's under the table, next to the dog."

"What about that boy?" my mother asked.

"He's not sitting at the table! He's with the dog! That painting is telling him his place. I want him at the table, sitting next to Jesus."

I was now screaming. My mother held my hand, calm.

WE FLEW TO ROME. I was done. My mother complained that her legs hurt. Every moment, every image felt like an omen—a bird flying across the sunset, making a glamorous exit; a woman riding a bike with her baby on the back. The woman hit a distracted pedestrian and fell.

I did not know what I thought would happen on this trip. Perhaps I thought we'd become different people, people untouched by loss. I wasn't even sure who I was trying to be, or become. I'd brought my mother clothes. I'd prepared her food. Clearly I wanted to flip the script, be the mother for her she hadn't been for me.

Yet I was also old enough to know that when you lose a mother at age six, part of you always remains a child, stays frozen as that girl wanting to jump onto her lap, yearning for her approval and for the false reassurance that she can protect you from the world.

I knew none of that would come true.

In Rome I became preoccupied with my mother recognizing my effort, with her seeing how well I'd planned this trip, thanking me for it. She'd communicated that she was grateful, but she kept praising God. God gave us these gifts. God created this moment. God made you and me.

"Yes, I see that, Mom," I said. "But why don't you also see that I'm making this experience for us? I created these moments."

"I see that, *mwana wanjye*," she said. "I see, and I appreciate it. But God . . ." After calling me *mwana wanjye*, my child, she slipped back into the comfort of her story—her Jesus, her heaven. "We're some of the luckiest people. The luckiest people. We have our whole family."

I WAS ON ONE SIDE of a giant chasm and my mother was on the other. We traveled together, parallel to each other, but we did not connect. Perhaps it was too much to ask.

It was like that with Claire too. I owe her my life. Every time I need to summon my toughest, most self-actualized persona, I channel her. She has such control, an unwavering sense of her right to exist, a bedrock belief that her story, no matter how dark, matters just as much as anyone else's, and she instilled that value in me. I wish Claire could appreciate her own uncanny ability to navigate a world that is constantly trying to push her down. But words have limits. I have none that adequately capture our knotted relationship. My most generous feelings are clouded by my own need to be recognized.

Not long ago, Claire came to visit me in San Francisco and I said, "I feel like you don't see me. I feel like you don't appreciate me and the work I've done."

I felt disregarded, unseen, by the one person in the

world who knew. "When you share about our experiences," I said to Claire, "you always say *I. I.* You don't say *we*. We were together."

"But you know," Claire said, "when I remember our experiences, I'm alone."

These days, when I'm with Claire, we have so much love and so much fear, and we want to kill each other. When she's home, in Chicago, instead of focusing on her own survival or mine, Claire wants to save her whole community, every refugee. Most Sundays she cooks for dozens of friends plus our family. "You are very stupid," one of these friends told her recently. "Why do you feed all these people? You're a single mother. You don't have money, and all these people come to your house?"

Claire doesn't live by that logic. "I've been doing this for a long time," she told her friend. "I have food, and I know I will have food tomorrow."

That was our mother's wisdom: Share. Cut the orange into more pieces. "Don't worry," my mother used to whisper when many people turned up unexpectedly at our table and our portions grew very small. "If you're not full at lunch, you'll be full tonight."

Claire's children knew enough to let Claire be, to let her live by her own inscrutable set of rules. That's all a person can do, really: Let others live their lives on their terms, and interrogate how you live your own. Insist on knowing the backstory to your gifts and your pain. Ask yourself how you came to have all the things you carry: your privilege, your philosophy, your nightmares, your faith, your sense of order and peace in the world.

Almost every January, Claire flew back to Rwanda. She

bought rice, beef, and potatoes so that she could prepare a big New Year's meal for orphans. Then she put on a fabulous dress, borrowed one of my aunt's most expensive bags, and made my aunt or my uncle, whoever was nearby, take hundreds of pictures of her—Claire's statement that *I am here. I am worthy and valuable. You did not destroy me.*

Back home in Chicago, scrolling through the images, Claire's youngest daughter always asked, incredulous, "How could you possibly do that?" *How could you do something that seems so frivolous in a place that caused so much pain?*

Claire saw no alternative. She just shrugged and said, "What do you want me to do? Cry?"

WE RETURNED TO CHURCH TOURISM—me and my mother in her new coat. On our last day in Rome we went to the Basilica of Saint Paul.

I wandered off to analyze the architecture, to get back to myself—to parse the building's history, to dissect its mechanics of awe. This felt like such a relief, to retreat into the world of symbolism, to calm myself with impersonal academic self-talk.

But after a moment, I shut that down and went to look for my mother. I found her speaking with two nuns, asking if they knew where Saint Brigid was.

"Yes, yes, she's in the sanctuary," one of the nuns said.

My mother, normally so controlled, could hardly contain her excitement. Saint Brigid is the saint of babies. If you needed to pray for a baby, you prayed to her.

The Basilica had a service going in the sanctuary, so we had to wait. When it ended, we walked in, and there she was, up in front in an alcove, above us. My mother knelt down and I knelt beside her. She lifted her eyes, clutched her rosary, and cried. "Sisters, you don't understand," my mother began telling the nuns. "My children, my girls, they were gone for seven years. I didn't know where they were. I prayed for the girls and that prayer was answered. They are here. My daughter is here."

I watched my mother's face. She appeared so content, so present, so glorious in that moment, complete in her miracle, holding her string of beads. Her faith had repaired the world. I was happy to be beside her. I envied the comfort she felt.

The next day we took a train back to the airport. We waited for our separate planes, drinking tea. I bought my mother an extra croissant to carry with her in her bag. I checked several times to be sure she had her passport.

She had a story that worked for her. I had only a character, a rubric. The girl who smiled beads gave me a way to go through the world, to believe in my own agency and my right to make decisions for myself, but I was still looking for a narrative that felt coherent and complete. No one was going to tell me the plot. It was not going to write itself. I still, *still,* after everything—Sebald, *Night,* all the *katundu,* the thousands of snapshots of my travels—longed for Mukamana. I wanted her to sit on the side of my bed, talk to me, and make my world feel not just magnificent but logical and whole.

I got on my plane, opened my notebook, and tried to go back to the start.

22

Not that long ago, in a land full of hills, not that far away, there lived two girls.

Every day, they played in their mother's garden. They wore yellow and red dresses and played among the brightest of flowers, and climbed trees with their brother. In the evenings, they brought their father his slippers, and asked him for treats at night. One day they heard noises that they'd never heard and saw expressions on their parents' faces that they'd never seen. The sky turned orange and the earth turned gray. They were sent to visit their grandmother, but they heard more noises and saw more strange faces and their grandmother told them to run.

They ran, and walked, and rode the bus, and nearly drowned on boats. They wandered for seven years, until the older sister was no longer a child and the younger sister wasn't either. They flew and they landed far away, and the younger sister tried to become a child again, even though she was far too hard to be a child. She looked for new parents. She looked for new powers. She read new books, and everywhere she went people thought she was magic.

People thought they knew her, people thought they saw her. As she passed by, they said, *She's so strong, she's so brave.* When she told her story they were even more impressed. *Poor girl, poor beautiful, special girl,* they said, and then they gave her gifts. She was given back her original parents. She was given shiny new siblings. She was given money, status, jewelry, praise, and the fanciest education in the world.

One day she dressed up like she did when she was a little girl and posed for photos in a beautiful garden. She sat with the geraniums, the lilies, and the birds-of-paradise, all the same flowers that her mother grew. She liked the feel of the sun on her skin. That alone—the warmth—made her feel nourished and whole. The colors all came back to her—only richer and deeper. She wore a red dress and then a happy yellow dress and then a dress with the orange she hated, the orange that filled the sky when she ran.

Each day she stared at her pictures—the flowers, her skin, the colors, her scars. She tried to hold in her head that it was all true: she was magic, beautiful, strong, brave, triumphant, and hurt. She tried to keep her memories in order, grounded in time. She wanted to tell a true story, a complete story. No ending ever felt right. History made it hard.

ACKNOWLEDGMENTS

FROM CLEMANTINE

I am so deeply grateful to each and every one of you. Thank you for sharing your lives with me, for seeing me, for welcoming me into the places and spaces that enabled me to reflect on and piece together parts of my life. I don't have words to express how you have enriched my perspective and my understanding of being alive. And to those I do not remember by name, who held me and spoke to me in the midst of chaos, I honor your kindness and gentleness. I am all of you, and I will pass forward the gifts you have shared with me.

To Claire: I thank Imana for adorning you with the love and strength to lead us through the highs and lows of our journey. Thank you for being patient with me and all my craziness. Your life is a gift, and the world and I owe you for sharing a small piece of it with us. I am looking forward to our next adventures.

To my mom, Christine Mukakalisa, and my dad, Appolinaire Ndayisaba: I am thankful for the lessons and examples you share, for your courage and your grace. I pray I live to love and share as you do.

To my other parents, MMB, Elizabeth Maxwell Thomas, PPB, and Frederick Thomas: Thank you for welcoming me into your life, and for your support, guidance, and lessons. Your kindness, love, and humility are a few of many gifts that I will cherish forever and pass forward.

Liz Weil, your openness and listening abilities are out of this planet. There are no words to express my gratitude for your commitment, your sacrifices, and the pure love you shared with me to create this book. Dan, thank you for making us delicious meals. Hannah, thank you for your encouragement and kindness. Audrey, thank you for sharing your sense of humor and keeping us on the tips of our toes.

Mark Lotto, I am glad I lost my phone at that Kickstarter party; otherwise, we wouldn't be where we are today. Thank you for sharing your time, creativity, and sense of wonder with me—and for your gift of seeing beyond words.

Maggie Grainger, I am humbled and thankful for every hour you spent listening to me and gathering every part of our lives into organized form.

Ian, I couldn't have done it without you. I could not have wished for a better partner to share this journey with. Thank you for listening, and for your kindness and patience. I am forever grateful for every minute and ounce of strength you shared with me.

To my agent, Kris Dahl at ICM: Thank you for your immense effort and for connecting the dots, especially to Liz. I am grateful for the time and energy you poured into making sure I had the support I needed to make this book possible. You are a star—thank you for sharing your spark with me.

To the entire team at Crown, each and every one of you: Thank you so much for every single little thing you did to make sure this book made it into the hands of readers. To my editor, Rachel Klayman: I appreciate you, your attention to detail, and your love for sharing stories that open our hearts. To my publisher, Molly Stern: I am grateful for your trust and enthusiasm; they were the glue that held me together throughout this process. Penny Simon and Lisa Erickson, thank you for your tremendous efforts to share the book with the world. Zach Phillips, thank you for keeping us organized.

Eric Brown and Michael Rudell, I am grateful to you for walking me through this process kindly and thoughtfully. Deborah Oppenheimer, thank you for honoring human journeys, for opening up new worlds to me, and especially for introducing me to Kris.

Michele, Dan, Julia, and Robert, you are incredible, thoughtful people whom anyone would wish to guide them into a new life. Michele, you saw me! Your influence has been the catalyst for so many unbelievable moments that led me to reflect and share. May Imana shower you with the gifts you have shared with me and many others, always.

Jill Weinberg, your passion and your commitment to bringing communities together has opened a passage to many rooms, where I have learned and felt the joy of being alive. Thank you for feeding me, nurturing me, and sharing your compassion.

To Tom, Andi, and the rest of the Bernsteins: You are the cheerleaders any girl would want after a Macy's parade. Your love and encouragement is out of this world, and I am thankful to you for welcoming me into your family. Tom, I am grateful for your foresight, guidance, and efforts to connect us to our human family.

To Mama Napele, Mama Dina, Papa Bilombele, Kasikile, Dina, Mwasiti, Mado, Patrick and Etienne, and Papa and Mama Fatuma: I salute your strength and everything you were able to share with me.

Wilma Kline, thank goodness for all our shopping, laughter, and silly moments. I needed that. To Donald Pasulka, Severa Mukamwiza, John and Jennifer Puisas, Sharon Vanderslice, Jim Graves, Vera Wells, Joshua Mbaraga, Amy and Andrew Cohen, Donna Gruskay, Betsy Blumenthal, Jonathan Root, Kevin King, Meridee Moore, Strive and Tsitsi Masiyiwa, Margaret and John Thornton, Lourdes, Pepe Fanjul Jr., Tina and Rick Malnati, and Andy and Kathy Gabelman: I hope you get a chance to meet one another soon. It is a blessing to know you and to be part of your lives. Thank you for all your support and mentorship, and for welcoming me into your homes. I'm so grateful for the kindness and gentleness you share with me and your communities.

To my sibs: Claudine, Claudette, Clement, Caulay, Stephen, Brad, Neely, Julia C. Robert, Perri, Julia, Sam, Will, Lee, Alexa, Matthew, Lindsay, Tanya, Vimbai, Joanna, Moses, Esther, Sarah, Max, Arthur, Eve, Amelia, Isabel, Kenneth,

Joel, Suzan, Lulu, and Peps: Love and thank you for sharing your parents with me. I'm sorry, you are stuck with me!

To my nieces and nephews, Mariette, Freddy, Michele, Chase, and Kate: You are my *bahati*.

To Ms. Oprah Winfrey: Thank you for envisioning our family reunion, for making it happen, and for sharing it with the world. I am also grateful to the Harpo/OWN team, Eric Peltier, Amanda Cash, and those whom I have yet to meet. Our efforts to share my family's story have enabled me to appreciate how important it is that we all share our experiences.

To Hannah Bogen, McKay Nield, (A)Lex Caron, Susannah Shattuck, Radha Mistry, Victoria Rogers, Amir Sharif, Zahra Baitie, Blair Miller, Tai Beauchamp, Alexandra Thornton, Abby West, Linda Lai, Benjamin Armstrong, Traci Kim, Hawa Hassan, Campbell Schnebly-Swanson, Patty Soffer, Katherine Maxwell, Alexandra Ivker, Aldi Kaza, Vicki, Hassan, Katie and Reed Colley, Ann Wolk Krouse, and Michael and Sheila Cohen. Thank you for laughing, crying, and dancing with me throughout this process.

To the people who inspire me every day: dream hampton, Danai Gurira, Nicole Patrice De Member, Zachary O. Enumah, Brenna Hughes Neghaiwi, Yemile Bucay, Julia Zave, Nina and Linda Friend, Maria O'Neill, Becky van der Bogert, Eileen Silva-Tetlow, Diego Taccioli, Kinari Webb, Peter Graves, Heather Scott Arora, John and Audra Hanusek, Michelle Musgrove Price, Wayne Price, Susan Lowenberg, Joyce Newstat, John W. Rogers Jr., Desirée Rogers, Galorah Keshavarz, Magatte Wade, Hank Thomas Willis, and Rujeko Hockley. Thank you for your magic and your support.

To my Manuscript fam, Dots, and my Summit family: Thank you for cheering me on, always.

To the Yale community: First and foremost, huge thanks to the Timothy Dwight team, especially for showing up in the winters. I am forever grateful for your time, your energy, and the smiles you shared with me after all-nighters in the library and the dining rooms. Diane Charney, you were my first editor, and I am sorry you had to read all my bad writing. Thank you for everything. Carolyn Barrett, Judith York, Karin Gosselink, and the rest of the writing center staff: Thank you for fighting for the resources that all of us who are differently abled need to be badass. Dean John Loge: My goodness, I have no idea if I would have survived Yale without our Friday visits. To Jeffrey Brenzel, for your wisdom, passion, and tremendous investment in our humanity. To the ladies who run TD, Patricia (Trish) Cawley and Karen McGovern: You have the most beautiful souls and energy that a college student could ever need. Carol Jacobs, Laura Wexler, Barbara Stuart, Mwalimu Kiarie Wa'Njogu, Katie Trumpener, J. Johnson, Ann Bier-Steker, and Elizabeth Rubin: Thank you for your encouragement and inspiration.

To the Hotchkiss School community: I am so grateful to you for welcoming all my craziness and for your patience with me when I broke the rules. To the staff, faculty, and students: You gave me an incredible opportunity to learn more about myself. Luisa Redetzki, I have no idea what I would have done without your straightforward, do-not-mess-with-me vibes. To the Wieler girls: Thank you for late-night dance parties and pizza. Sofia Zafra, thank you for all the colors, flowers, and love for your country. Professor Louis Pressman, Simon Walker, Jennifer Craig, Christina Cooper, Alice Sarkissian-Wolf, J. Bradley Faus, and Damon White: Thank you for asking more of me in my thoughts, creativity, and well-being.

To the New Trier School community: Hilerre Kirsch, Nina Lynn, Marie Adelaide, Cathy D'Agostino, Jeannie Lee Logan, Laura Deutsch, and all the art and ESL teachers. Thank you for sharing your gifts with me. You laid a great foundation that allowed me to understand different aspects of American culture and survive those long hallways.

To the North Shore Country Day community: I'm so grateful to each and every one of you for your love and continuing support for my family. Kathy McHugh, Barbara Sherman, and Anne-Marie Dall'Agata: Your joy in teaching and sharing your knowledge is out of this world. Please continue.

To the Swift School and Christian Heritage Academy communities: I don't remember most of your full names, since I didn't speak or understand much English when I knew you. Ms. Garcia, Anayeli, Donika, Sharon James Ledbetter, the Beasley family: You had a huge impact on my first years in America. Thank you for communicating your truth and love without words.

To the Body Temp Yoga team, Heather Piper, Christie Rafanan, Brenna Barry, and Chadd Schaefer: Thank you for reminding me to pause, breathe, and sweat it all out.

To the storytellers who enabled me to find the beats and rhythm of my words, including many I know only through your art: Mukamana, Mucyechuru and Musaza, Nina Simone, Audre Lorde, Maya Angelou, Toni Morrison, Ruby Sales, Chinua Achebe, Elie Wiesel, W. G. Sebald, Hayao

Miyazaki, and others who live in my ways of being. Your sense of wonder has been a ticket to this adventure. Thank you for helping me to hear my own heartbeat and breath, and to see beyond labels.

To my communities all over the world, those of you who share and who teach me how to expand and deepen my ways of seeing, hearing, touching, tasting, and smelling all that keeps us alive. Thank you.

FROM ELIZABETH

I will forever be profoundly grateful to you, Clemantine, for the chance to work together on this. Thank you for trusting me.

Claire, it's been an amazing gift to have you in my life as well. I hope I've done justice to yours.

Deep gratitude to Rachel Klayman and Molly Stern at Crown, for their unwavering belief in this book and their intense commitment to share it with the world; to Mark Lotto, for his vision and care from start to finish; to Kris Dahl, for insisting that I at least meet Clemantine for coffee; to Elyse Cheney, for sticking up for me; to Julie Tate, for saving me from my own mistakes; to Maggie Grainger, for listening; to Amelia Zalcman, for vetting; to Harvey Schwartz, for helping me understand; to Dick Duane, for going far beyond the call of any father-in-law.

To the Thomases, for treating me like family; and to Joshua, Vicki, and Hassan, for showing me Rwanda.

To Inga Davis, Anton Krukowski, Mark Lukach, Wendy MacNaughton, Emily Newman, and Maria Streshinsky, for reading and providing incredible feedback.

To Taffy Brodesser-Akner, for reading not only chapters but also endless texts and hysterical emails, and for shouldering the emotional burden as only a wife could. Your friendship saw me through.

To Hannah, for reading and for still wanting to be a writer, and for making me incredibly proud; to Audrey, for exhaustively searching for a title and for not wanting to be a writer, and for buoying my heart; to both of them, for putting up with a grumpy mother. To my parents, for supporting me, always.

Dan, I love you utterly. Thank you, always, for everything.

ABOUT THE AUTHORS

Clementine Wamariya is a storyteller and human rights advocate. Born in Kigali, Rwanda, and displaced by conflict, Clementine migrated through seven African countries as a child. At age twelve, she was granted refugee status in the United States and went on to receive a B.A. in comparative literature from Yale University. She lives in San Francisco.

Elizabeth Weil is a writer-at-large for the *New York Times Magazine* and a contributing editor to *Outside* magazine, and she writes frequently for *Vogue* and other publications. She is the recipient of a New York Press Club Award for her feature reporting, a Lowell Thomas Award for her travel writing, and a GLAAD Media Award for her coverage of LGBT issues. In addition, her work has been a finalist for a National Magazine Award, a James Beard Award, and a Dart Award for coverage of trauma. She lives in San Francisco with her husband and two daughters.

THE GIRL WHO SMILED BEADS

EXTRA
LIBRIS

ESSAYS,
READER'S GUIDES,
AND MORE

A Conversation with
Clemantine Wamariya

Q. In 1994, when you were six years old, you and
your fifteen-year-old sister had to flee Rwanda
very suddenly, carrying almost nothing. How
did you get from that moment to where you are
now?

A. It's taken a lot of years for me to learn how to share
my story. It's painful, still, for me to go back to that
day. My sister and I had been sent to our grandmother's house to keep us safe because the civil war in
Rwanda had moved to a new level and soldiers were
beginning to massacre people. One day there was a
knock on the door and our grandmother motioned
for us to run out the back toward a sweet potato field.
We never saw our home again. From that point on,
the world fell away and nothing made sense. Over the
next six years we wandered through seven different
African countries, through hunger and fear, and moments of unexpected beauty, too. My sister saved us,
again and again. In 2000, when I was twelve, she got
us asylum in the United States, and we started on a
whole different journey.

Q. The title of your book comes from a story your nanny told you as a young girl. Why, of all the stories she told you, do you think that one stayed so clear in your mind through the years?

A. That story was magic! When my nanny, Mukamana, told me about the girl who smiled beads, she did not just lay out the plot. She invited me to shape the tale. She set out this character, this miraculous, beautiful girl who smiled beads. Then she set that girl in the world—first in her mother's house, then walking the earth—and each step of the way Mukamana asked, "What do you think happened next?" Whatever I said, Mukamana told me I was right. The story allowed me to believe I controlled my own destiny. It allowed me to try to make sense of a universe I could not understand. By the time I was six, the universe had turned upside down. Neighbors were disappearing, soldiers were murdering families. I understood so little. What were borders? Why did people hate us? Why did we need papers to flee war and seek peace?

The girl who smiled beads also spoke to me in a very deep way about self-worth. I so badly wanted to be that girl. Inside she had an abundance of treasure. She took it with her everywhere she went and it never ran out. The world tried so hard, for so many years, to tell me and my sister, Claire, that we were worthless. That story proved them wrong. I am a treasure to the world. My value is limitless. No one can take that away.

Q. As a child, what were the first signs you noticed that the world as you knew it was in jeopardy?

A. I was so young at the time, so as the world imploded I noticed small things in what, for me, was still a very small, safe world. I heard drumming in the streets. I saw expressions on my parents' faces I'd never seen before. My mother stopped going to the church and instead prayed at home. My father stopped going to work. I had a sleepover with a friend, and we traded sweaters as we were parting ways, and then I never saw her again to trade back. My mother drew the shades in our house. I asked my brother about strange noises. He told me the gunshots were thunder.

Q. You and Claire lived in several refugee camps—in Burundi, Tanzania, Malawi, and Mozambique. What was the day-to-day reality like for you in those situations?

A. You wait in line for corn, for hours. You wait in line for water. You pick bugs out of your feet. You are in a constant battle against lice. The whole environment is constructed to strip your identity away. I tried so hard to hold onto myself. I was telling everybody—and to be honest, myself—"I'm Clemantine! I'm Clemantine! I'm Clemantine!" The only thing I was expert on when I arrived at our first camp, in Burundi, was being a well-cared-for little girl. Many of the kids in the camp walked around naked and filthy and that threw me into a rage. I could not stand to see the flies around their eyes that nobody bothered to swat. I screamed at them, "Where is your mother? Get out of here and go tell your mother to put clothes on you." Of course, at that moment, I had no mother to clothe me myself. But I did find loving, intact people who shared their hearts and lives with me. One older couple took me into the forest beside the camp to hunt for mushrooms with them. They taught me to treat all living things, including every plant, with deep respect. One day we found a green tomato. It was spectacular! I hadn't seen a tomato in months.

Q. In the first chapter, you say of your sister: "I have never been Claire. I have never been inviolable." How did her response to the challenges of refugee life differ from yours? How did you make a good team, and what did you struggle over?

A. Claire is the real hero of this story. She saved my life, again and again, and from the start she had this unshakable understanding that no matter how hard our lives got, no matter how thoroughly the world tried to break her down, nobody got to take her dignity. That was hers and she was never giving it away. She always made sure she had one decent outfit—jeans and a pressed white shirt—so everywhere we went she could present herself as an equal and command not pity but respect. She was also just incredible at the hustle of our refugee life. She walked out of one camp, bought a goat, pulled it back to the camp on a rope, found a man who knew how to butcher it, gave him the goat's head for his troubles, and sold the rest of the meat. My role in our lives was pretty different. Claire had her first baby when I was eight. I was still a child myself but I took care of Claire's kids. Sometimes I felt she did not appreciate what I did for them, but now that I'm older I see that she had such an incredible burden herself finding us food and shelter.

Q. Soon after you arrived in the United States, you were taken in and treated like a daughter by an American family living in the Chicago suburbs. What surprised you most about their world? What were the hardest things to adjust to in the United States?

A. The Thomas family showed me such unbelievable kindness. I was kind of paralyzed at first. I loved the fancy soaps in the downstairs bathrooms. I was utterly bewildered at first by Ginger, their pet dog, because in Rwanda nobody treated dogs like people! Mrs. Thomas, in particular, was so gentle and patient with me. She taught me how to read. She made my lunches. She drove me and picked me up from school. When I arrived in the United States at age twelve I was already an adult. I became an adult the moment we ran. Mrs. Thomas allowed me to be a child again.

Q. You describe feeling electrified by reading Elie Wiesel's Holocaust memoir *Night* when you were in eighth grade. Why did that book mean so much to you?

A. *Night* was the door that opened up the world for me. That is truly not an exaggeration. The book made me feel not crazy. It made me feel not alone. Wiesel had words to express experiences I couldn't articulate. He shared thoughts and feelings that I was too ashamed to name. Nobody had told me what happened in Rwanda and I was too young when I was there to understand the destruction of my whole world. It's an honor and a privilege to publish a book, and it's the result of so many people believing in and investing in me. If one person can have the reading experience I had with *Night* with my book, all the pain of remembering and writing (and there was a lot!) will have been worth it. Since that time I've had so many amazing experiences with books— W. G. Sebald's *Austerlitz,* Maya Angelou's *Phenomenal Woman*, Audre Lorde's *Sister Outsider.*

Q. During the time when you were moving from country to country in Africa, you had to adapt to circumstances and expectations in order to survive, and you became incredibly good at decoding what others needed and wanted from you. Now that you've been in the United States for nearly seventeen years, how do you think about your identity and situate yourself in the world around you?

A. Describing myself is not one of my strengths! I used to feel so frustrated that I couldn't produce a simple description of who I am or even what I do. But I recently made peace with this. Who I am and what I'm doing depends on who I am with. As a child, I learned to adapt. I had to. And even now, I place a lot of value on place and circumstance and interpersonal exchanges. For example, I have a friend who spends most of the day cleaning Chestnut Street, a very busy commercial strip near the bay in San Francisco. Every time we see each other, we stop, talk, and find something to smile about. To Calvin, I am the girl on Chestnut

Street with a yoga mat who pauses to laugh and chat. I don't need to be a Yale grad or a humanitarian or a former refugee to him. It's better to just connect as two people sharing a street. Refusing to be frozen as a particular character is now a practice to me. It allows me to try to be intimate and equal with everybody.

Q. You write about obsessively collecting stuff—beads and other artifacts that mean something to you. What did possessions mean to you during your years of flight? What have you chosen to save over the years in the United States?

A. When Claire and I were moving from country to country, without our parents, looking for safety, I collected rocks from the different places we stayed. I hoped I would see my mother again and that I could show her where I'd been. I also collected marbles for my brother, Pudi, who didn't flee with us. I kept all my stuff—my *katundu*—in a Mickey Mouse backpack that I had received as a gift in Zaire. I loved that backpack. It was my lifeline, my identity summed up in a bunch of marbles and rocks. One night we fled Malawi to go to Mozambique. During that journey I left it on a bus. I could still cry every time I think about that backpack. I went to Disneyland about fifteen years later, when I was a junior at Yale, interning at Google for the summer. In a small way, being there—seeing men and women in Mickey and Minnie suits—made me feel whole. Now, I collect almost everything—every ticket stub, every birthday card. It's really a problem. Trauma leaves you with a fractured memory. My stuff helps me hold on to and make sense of who I am.

Q. When you were a junior in high school, you were reunited with your parents live on the Oprah show. When you saw them walk out onto the Oprah stage, a moment you had "fantasized about . . . so many times," what went through your mind? How did the experience of being reunited evolve after the initial shock?

A. It was completely surreal. Seeing my mother and father come through that door, it was as if they had come back from the dead. My parents also, by that point, had more children, which meant I had brand-new siblings I'd never met. I felt so much joy and so much anger. I felt like I'd been given the most beautiful hug and a kick in the gut at the same time. Time and space had robbed us of so much. We knew our parents were alive by that point but we hadn't seen them in seven years and we'd barely communicated. Right after the taping we all went into the green room to have some time alone. Nobody knew what to say. After the years apart, where do you start? Claire was frozen—not smiling, not crying, a mannequin. You can't just staple your family together again.

Q. When you achieved a place at an elite boarding school, and then Yale, you describe feeling energized by things you were learning but also feeling deeply alienated. In what ways did you feel alienated by your classes and fellow students, and why?

A. I am incredibly grateful for the education I've been given, but there were times, especially at Hotchkiss, when I felt so out of place. I took a philosophy seminar during which the professor asked the students to game out a scenario: "You're a ferryboat captain. The ship is sinking. How do you decide who lives and who dies?" That was not a hypothetical question to me. I've been in a boat so overloaded with desperate humans fleeing starvation and war that people had to start throwing their luggage into the water so we didn't all sink and die. I lost it in that class and started screaming, "You have no idea, do you? You've never been in that scenario. What gives you the right to even talk? This is real. That's me—and I have a name and I'm alive and there are people out there who are dead, or they're living but they're checked out and they hate the world because people in your country sat there and watched all of us getting slaughtered."

Q. There's a striking passage in the book where you write: "When I'm angry, I think in Swahili because that's the language in which I learned to fully express my emotions." What Swahili words describe your emotions about publishing this book? And is there an equivalent English translation?

A. *Haraka haraka haina baraka.* It's a bit hard to translate. Literally it means, *Fast fast, there is no luck.* The point is, if you're in a hurry, you'll miss out on the good stuff. Writing this book and releasing it into the world is thrilling, but there's a panic to it. I feel like I've been in pieces for months! I worked so slowly for years, on my survival, on my education, on reading and writing. And now, my goodness, it feels like such a rush. *Haraka haraka haina baraka.* That's my reminder to myself to try to slow down. I want to take a moment and enjoy it. This book is about so many people and the result of so many people sharing with me. If I rush, I fear I'll miss out on all I have to learn from the experience of sharing the book with the world.

Q. The importance of the language we use to tell our stories—as well as its limits—is a central theme in the book. For example, you write about your intense dislike of the word *genocide*. Why do you dislike the word so much?

A. I hate the word *genocide*. It's so distancing and antiseptic, a performance, the worst kind of lie. It captures absolutely nothing about my experience. It tells you nothing about how it feels when you know the world wants you dead and you don't even understand what death is yet. I also truly hate the word *refugee*. It lumps together and flattens so many individual human lives. I am not a refugee. I sought refuge for many years, but the word *refugee* does not define me. It just limits me and puts me in a box.

Q. You write that when people hear you talk about your experience: "Some wanted to help me, and could not stand the idea that I was not defeated. Panic flashed across their faces when I suggested . . . that I could help them too." What do you mean by this?

A. Not everybody wants to believe they share equal humanity and equal value with a person who has been introduced to them as a refugee and genocide survivor. People want to give, which is a very nice impulse, but giving in one direction—you give to me, I do not give to you—maintains the power status quo. Sharing is very different. Sharing presumes and creates equality. To me, this is one of the most important ideas in the book. You might have time and I might have land. You might have ideas and I might have strength. You might have a tomato and I might have a knife. We need each other. We need to say: I am not better than you. You are not better than me. Nobody is better than anybody else.

Q. Do you talk about what happened in Rwanda with your sister or your parents?
A. No. We live in the present together. My mother cooks for everybody every Sunday. We cannot talk with each other about the past, in words. We speak in actions. Someday Claire may wish to tell her own story. Right now she doesn't want to excavate the past—she wants to be with her people, support those who've walked the path she's walked, and build her life.

Q. What's the focus of your life moving forward?
A. I am deeply committed to finding joy in my life and living in the present right now. I want to listen to people's stories and find strength in them. There is so much human-caused pain and suffering in the world. I want to honor all those difficult experiences and acknowledge their aftermath. At the same time, I want to really see and love the world around me.

A Reader's Guide

Questions and Topics for Discussion

1. The title of the book is taken from a story Clemantine's nanny, Mukamana, tells her as a child. How is the story connected to the themes of the book?

2. After fleeing Rwanda, Clemantine fears losing her sense of self in refugee camps. In what ways does her longing to preserve her individuality express itself?

3. In the first chapter of the book, Clemantine tells us: "I have never been Claire. I have never been inviolable." As the story unfolds, she and her sister react to trauma in very different ways, and rely on different survival strategies. How would you characterize their differences? Which events best illustrate those differences?

4. Clemantine's experience as a "stateless" person is harrowing, yet there are times when she and her sister experience great kindness and generosity. Describe some of the kindnesses that stood out to you.

5. Why do Clemantine's sister and mother instruct her not to accept gifts? And why does Clemantine come to see acts of charity as a negative thing? Do you agree with her view of charity?

6. Clemantine sets forth an alternative to charity, an ethic of sharing. What are the origins of this practice in her life?

7. The authors write: "In Rwanda, if you're female, you are born with great value—not because of who you are as an individual or your mind, but because of your body." What do they mean by that? How has that mindset affected Clemantine's life, both during the time she was seeking refuge and in the United States? Do you see any parallels to this attitude about the female body in your own culture?

8. After she arrives in the United States, there are times when Clemantine feels alienated by American culture. What is most surprising to her about American culture? What are some of the things that make her uncomfortable or anger her?

9. Clemantine takes issue with the word *genocide,* which she describes as "clinical, overly general, bloodless, and dehumanizing." In her view, that one word cannot adequately capture the atrocities of racialization and war in Rwanda. Do you agree that words and abstract concepts can distort or overwrite people's experience? Are there words about which you feel similarly?

10. Clemantine sometimes speaks at events about being a survivor of genocide. In some ways she finds it rewarding but more often she finds it unsatisfying. What is it that she finds objectionable and why?

11. Clemantine writes about how important her *katundu,* or stuff, is to her. What do you think the objects she collects represent to her? What cherished objects have you saved, and what do they mean to you?

12. Clemantine talks about how meaningful the works of Elie Wiesel, Toni Morrison, Maya Angelou, James Baldwin, Walter Benjamin, and W. G. Sebald have been for her. In what ways did these writers equip her to grapple with her past, her pain, and her feelings of loneliness and isolation? In what ways did they expand her worldview? Who are the writers whose work has been most valuable to you in making sense of difficult events of your own past?

13. Clemantine goes on a trip to Kenya with fellow students when she is at Yale, but she ends up returning early. What does she find difficult about the trip?

14. Clemantine describes returning to Rwanda for Remembrance Day, where the government has an official historical narrative, seen in the Kigali Genocide Memorial and President Kagame's speech. Describe the Rwandan government's version of the country's history. In what ways does this narrative give Rwandan people "a way to tolerate an intolerable truth"?

15. Claire tells Clemantine: "Everything is yours, everything is not yours. The world owes you nothing; nobody deserves more or less than the next person." What does she mean by that? If those values were universally practiced, how might our society and the global community look different?

16. Why do Clemantine and Claire feel so differently about the adage "forgive and forget"? Do you believe in forgiving and forgetting wrongs that have been done to you?

17. Why do you think the authors chose to structure the book so that it oscillates between Clemantine's time in Africa and her life after emigrating to the United States, rather than as a linear story?